The
Wealthy
Barber
Returns

Library and Archives Canada Cataloguing in Publication

Chilton, David Barr, 1961–

    The wealthy barber returns : significantly older and marginally wiser, Dave
    Chilton offers his unique perspectives on the world of money / David Chilton.

Includes bibliographical references.

Issued also in electronic and audio formats.

ISBN 978-0-9683947-4-8

1. Finance, Personal. I. Title.

HG179.C46 2011   332.024'01   C2010-907932-9

Edited by Susan Chilton and Fina Scroppo
Book design and production by WeMakeBooks.ca
Cover photographed by Terry Manzo

All inquiries should be addressed to:

 Financial Awareness Corp.
2 –1241 Weber St. E., Kitchener, Ontario N2A 1C2
519-747-2298 • 1-800-665-3913
www.wealthybarber.com
dchilton@wealthybarber.com

If you're interested in bulk purchases of *The Wealthy Barber Returns*, we offer an aggressive discount schedule. Please call us at one of the above numbers.

Printed in Canada

 Printed on 100% post-consumer recycled paper

The Wealthy Barber Returns

Significantly Older
and Marginally Wiser,
Dave Chilton Offers
His Unique Perspectives
on the World of Money

Dedication

I'VE MADE A LOT OF MISTAKES in my life, but for reasons beyond my control, I somehow managed to follow the best advice ever given: "Choose your parents wisely!" My mom and dad have been, and continue to be, hugely positive influences on me. As important, they are the ultimate grandparents to my children, providing not only unconditional love and support, but also strong examples of living with integrity. To my dismay, however, in their retirement years they've spent a tremendous amount of their hard-earned money on trips to far-off lands, lessening my potential inheritance considerably. I have pointed out that the Discovery Channel in high def is as good as being there, yet off they go on another cruise or tour. Nobody's perfect...but they're close! So, for all they've done for me, I dedicate this book to my mom and dad. This, despite the fact that after *The Wealthy Barber* became successful, my shocked father, when asked in an interview whether he and my mom were worried that I would be "a one-hit wonder," responded, "That's one hit more than we thought he'd have."

Introduction

UNTIL RECENTLY, I BELIEVED I would never write another personal-finance book. Luck played such a huge role in *The Wealthy Barber*'s success that I didn't want to tempt fate.

So what changed my mind?

Frustration.

After watching Canadians' savings rates plunge, debt levels sky-rocket and investment returns consistently disappoint over the last decade, I was pulling my hair out. I wondered, "How can I help?"

I'm hopeful that *The Wealthy Barber Returns* will answer that question.

Although it doesn't use its predecessor's novel format (yes, that's a generous use of the word "novel"), this, too, is an unusual financial-planning book.

There are no checklists, no graphs and almost no charts. Heck, there's hardly any math.

Essentially, it's just me chatting casually about the world of money. It's almost as though I'm in your living room except better because, well, I'm not.

I'll admit that *The Wealthy Barber Returns* is certainly not comprehensive. Neither my knowledge nor a mere 200 pages would allow for that.

And by no means is it the definitive word on how to manage your finances. (Sadly, that doesn't exist.) In fact, you might disagree with some of my opinions — I'm sure that many in the industry will.

But I'm confident that what follows will make you think differently and more wisely about your saving, spending, borrowing and investment decisions.

In a way, I've been writing this book for more than 20 years. I really hope you enjoy and benefit from its ideas.

Even if you don't, though, please tell others that you did.

Dave

P.S. Yes, I know *The Wealthy Barber Returns* isn't the most creative title. My daughter asked, "What's next, Dad? *The Wealthy Barber Goes to Hawaii*? It's like the old *Gidget* series." I closed her RESP.

Contents

Random Thoughts on Personal Finance

Insights into
Saving, Spending
and Borrowing

A Painful Truth and
a Positive Spin

I HATE TO BEGIN WITH A DOSE of harsh reality, but here goes.

Unless you marry into wealth or come from a very well-to-do family (both highly advisable strategies, by the way), you'll have to learn to spend less than you make.

No, this isn't a tremendous insight and, yes, you've probably heard it a thousand times before but, unfortunately, that doesn't make it any less true. I never apologize for focusing on this simple teaching because (1) it's the absolute key to successful financial planning and (2) despite the fact it's oft-heard and self-evident, it clearly hasn't sunk in with the majority of Canadians. A disturbing number of us aren't saving enough to fund our future goals, most notably, a reasonable retirement.

However, let's stay positive here: Yes, we struggle as savers but we're absolutely fantastic spenders. So, instead of lamenting our inability to save, let's celebrate our incredible ability to spend!

In macroeconomic studies (don't worry, this will be painless), the following formula is used:

$$DY = C + S \quad \text{where}$$

DY is Disposable Income
C is Consumption (a fancy word for spending)
S is Savings

In other words, every after-tax dollar we receive can either be spent (consumed) or saved. Guess which option most of us choose over and over again? Bingo. For many Canadians, the more accurate formula is:

$$DY = C \quad \text{S has been completely Shunned.}$$

The bottom line is we love C! C is fun. S is boring. C is living in the moment. S is that rainy-day crap. C is high-definition TVs, hot tubs and fancy wine. S is discipline, unfulfilled desires and deferred gratification.

Really, C stands for Carpe diem. S stands for Sacrifice.

Why do we choose C? Better question: Why wouldn't we?

Long live C! Death to S!

Ah, but there's a major problem with that understandable and very prevalent attitude.

There's a breakdown in logic. Remember, later in life we'll all stop working. Our DY (Disposable Income, to remind you) will no longer come from our employment income — it will have to come from our S.

No S means no DY. No DY means no C. No C means no...well, let's not even think about that.

Maybe S isn't so bad after all! It may stand for Sacrifice during our working years, but during our retirement it stands for Salvation.

You see, the equation $DY = C + S$ gives the false impression that C and S, Consumption and Savings, are competitors fighting over DY's spoils. Perhaps in our C-oriented minds they are, but in reality they should be partners trying to split DY in a way that keeps C high enough to enjoy life now but also funds S enough to provide a good lifestyle later.

As is so often the case, it's all about balance. And the good news? Achieving the appropriate balance usually doesn't require dramatic lifestyle changes.

Honestly.

Let's say that you're currently saving four percent of your Disposable Income (DY).

So, knowing from earlier that DY = C + S, we can say:

$$\$1.00 = \$0.96 + \$0.04$$

(For every after-tax dollar you receive, you're spending 96 cents and saving 4 cents.)

Now some annoying financial advisor explains that based on your goals, pension details, age, etc., you'll have to raise your savings rate to at least 10 percent. "That's crazy!" you exclaim. "We can barely save the four percent — there's no way we can save two-and-a-half times as much. More than double our savings? Not happening!"

"You're right," the advisor concedes. "Let's forget that idea and focus on your spending. Instead of trying to raise your savings rate dramatically, a seemingly impossible goal, do you think you could start by cutting your spending rate by a mere 6.25 percent?"

"Yes, that seems much more reasonable," you allow.

Well, as you now know:

$$DY = C + S$$

Therefore, your new equation is:

$$\$1.00 = \$0.90 + \$0.10$$

How did I get that? Well, $0.90 is 6.25 percent less than $0.96 (6/96 = 0.0625 = 6.25%).

Amazingly, you've raised your savings rate by 150 percent simply by cutting your spending by only 6.25 percent.

It's a money miracle! (OK, that's a bit strong, but you have to admit, it is kinda cool.)

So, there's bad news and good news here. The bad news is that you have to save — sorry, but you must learn to live within your means. The good news is that a relatively small cutback in your spending rate can dramatically increase your savings rate. You don't have to become a miser and live a life of austerity. You just have to exercise a little discipline and a little common sense.

You're probably wondering, "If that's the case, why aren't there more successful savers? Why haven't we all been able to slightly reduce our spending?"

The blunt answer? A little discipline and a little common sense are a little more than most of us can muster.

Your Opponents

ONE OF THE BIGGEST REASONS that it's so difficult to save is that no one out there really wants you to.

It's true. Almost everyone wants you to spend as much as possible.

Your kids, if you have any, are constantly asking for the latest and greatest. They're relentless, cute and innately skilled in the art of manipulation — a powerful combination.

Friends are always suggesting a dinner out, buying a new toy that tempts you to do the same or inviting you to their wedding in Punta Cana. (Remember when everyone's reception was at a Legion hall?)

Your real-estate agent thinks you should extend your budget just a little bit: "Sure, it's more house than you need, but you'll grow into it. Besides, it's a once-in-a-lifetime opportunity. I really don't know what the listing agent was thinking pricing it so low!"

Bankers — well, the more you spend, the more they can lend. And lending is their raison d'être.

Any government's re-election (always its top priority) hinges on a strong economy, and its most important measure, gross domestic product (GDP), is determined primarily by consumer spending. A surging savings rate would scare the heck out of incumbents.

7

When the economies of developed nations recently crashed due to excessive private debts, governments responded by lowering interest rates and offering other incentives to get us to borrow and spend even more. This is akin to beginning an alcoholic's rehabilitation by sending him or her on a pub-crawl.

Clothiers, restaurateurs, car salespeople, furniture-store owners, spa managers, wholesale-club staffs, entertainment-industry executives, tourism boards — they're all, for good reason, non-stop cheerleaders exhorting us to part with our hard-earned dollars. And, frankly, our instant-gratification-oriented minds aren't putting up much resistance. "I deserve it" has become many people's mantra.

The bottom line is that when it comes to saving, you don't have much of a support group. There are really only three Canadians who want you to set aside some money — your future you, your financial advisor and me.

With the teams stacked against you, spending less than you make won't be easy. People are going to fight you every step of the way. And the person who will fight you the hardest will be yourself.

The good news, though, is that it is still possible to live within your means. You can learn a lot from those who do it — and even more from those who don't!

Consumed With Consumption

OBVIOUSLY, THERE ARE CERTAIN basic needs we all share — shelter, food and clothing being the big three.

Naturally, in a wealthy, developed economy like Canada's, our desires will run well beyond our stream of needs into our pool of wants.

That's understandable, even healthy. Our quest for "the good life," and the possessions and experiences it brings, is part of what motivates us to work hard, innovate, embrace risks, grow our talents and then take full advantage of them.

Plus, what's the point in achieving economic growth — either as a society or as an individual — if you can't enjoy some of the spoils?

I get that. I have a hot tub. And I love it. Really love it.

However, I think we can all agree that we've gone a little too far (actually, *a lot* too far) in our pursuit of stuff.

Nothing is ever enough. We want more. And when we get it, we want more yet again. We want what we see on TV. We want what our friends have. Heck, we want what rich people have. We even want what we already have but in the newer, fancier, bigger models.

We want with such emotional intensity that we're able to convince ourselves that our desires aren't wants at all, but instead integral components of our future happiness.

Nothing could be further from the truth.

In reality, all our stuff weighs us down. And our pursuit of "more" often distracts us from what's truly important in life. No, I'm not having an Oprah moment here. I genuinely believe that our never-ending material quest is not only sabotaging our financial tomorrows, but also negatively impacting our psychological todays.

The brilliant philosopher Bertrand Russell once noted, "It is preoccupation with possessions, more than anything else, that prevents us from living freely and nobly."

I couldn't have said it better myself (which is, of course, why I quoted him). One of the most damaging misconceptions in personal finance is that saving for the future requires sacrifices today that lessen people's enjoyment of life. Surprisingly, it's quite the opposite! People who live within their means tend to be happier and less stressed. That's true not only for the obvious reason — they know their financial futures look bright — but also because they're not consumed with consumption. They're not in the emotionally and financially draining race to acquire the most stuff they possibly can. A race that, it should be noted, has no finish line and thus no winner.

Too many people are possessed by their possessions. As Seneca said 2,000 years ago, "These individuals have riches just as we say that we have a fever, when really the fever has us."

Status Update

THE WORD "STATUS," NOT SURPRISINGLY, has Latin roots. (My dad, by the way, reads Latin. How cool is that? Useless, mind you, but cool nonetheless.) It comes from the Latin word *statum*, meaning standing — not as in standing up, but as in one's ranking. In other words, one's status is a reflection of one's importance in the eyes of others.

Most of us crave status. Almost all of us care greatly about what others think of us. Psychologists have long lamented this situation and remind us how potentially unhealthy it is to have our self-esteem so directly determined by the perceptions of others.

No argument there.

That being said, with status come flattery, social opportunities, respect for our opinions and attention. You know — all that horrible stuff. Higher status? Bring it on!

The problem, from a financial-planning perspective at least, isn't so much that we seek status — that's human nature — but rather how status has come to be awarded. Far too often, society now grants status based almost exclusively on a very narrow definition of success. This definition pays woefully little attention to one's family life, community involvement or even impact on others. Instead, it focuses on one variable: perceived wealth.

When you hear that John is "very successful," what jumps to mind? He's a great parent? He lives a balanced life? He's a man of character? Of course not. We all think the same thing: "Wow, John's makin' the big bucks!"

Even parents, subconsciously I hope, are often guilty of making "successful" synonymous with "financially successful." Many times I've asked someone, "How are the kids doing?" and received responses such as, "Mary is a successful dentist and Fred's a struggling mechanic." Perhaps Fred is a dud around cars and somehow his mom and dad found out (through RateYourMechanics.com, I suppose), but more likely, they're letting their children's incomes determine their adjectives.

What's more, we even mismeasure this mismeasurement. We gauge people's financial successes not by their net-worth statements (that would be bad enough — and tough to get at), but instead by their material possessions.

Is it any wonder conspicuous consumption rules?

Many of our purchases are made with others in mind, whether we realize it or not. From the sizes of our homes to the logos on our clothes to the brands of our cars, we're trying to make a statement about ourselves and, at its core, that statement is very basic: "Look at me — I'm worthy."

Ben Franklin said it best: "It is the eyes of others and not our own eyes which ruin us. If all the world were blind except myself I should not care for fine clothes or furniture."

Geoffrey Miller, one of the foremost experts in evolutionary psychology, assesses the situation more bluntly: "Modern consumers in particular strive to be self-marketing minds, feeding one another hyperbole about how healthy, clever, and popular they are, through the goods and services they consume."

Few things in life are more valuable than our self-esteem, yet we often willingly surrender it to the opinions of others. Then we spend a king's ransom trying to get it back.

As shallow and financially damaging as that is, as I said earlier, it's quite understandable. Fending off our biological wiring, societal pressures and deeply ingrained habits isn't easy. Alain de Botton, in his outstanding book *Status Anxiety*, concludes, "The most profitable way of addressing the condition may be to attempt to understand and to speak of it."

By the way, if you didn't enjoy this section, please don't let me know. The criticism might push me to buy something expensive.

Faulty Wiring

AFTER A SPEECH I GAVE A FEW years ago, a young woman told me about her struggle to save money. "I'm very good at delaying delayed gratification," she explained with a smile. We can all relate. Temptation is, well, very tempting.

Recent collaborations between neuroscientists (smart people who study our brains) and economists (boring people who study our economy) have shed some light on why we so often make decisions that are inconsistent with our long-term goals.

The "neuroeconomists" argue that our brain is of two minds, so to speak. One includes the prefrontal cortex, the parietal cortex and the temporal lobes. These are the parts of the brain that help us reason logically and plan. All of these areas are much larger in humans than in other animals (yes, including your brother-in-law). Neuroscientists have concluded these were the last components of the brain to evolve. Experts sometimes use the word "executive" to describe this area because it directs calm, reasoned decisions.

Beneath our executive sits what's known as our "lizard" — the oldest part of our brain, dating back to when we were, supposedly, reptiles. It includes our limbic system, insular cortex, striatum and amygdala — things I'd never heard of until, as your faithful financial scribe, I read study after study about how neural wiring affects our decision-making. The lizard responds to emotions and immediate needs and desires. It avoids pain and seeks pleasure. In general, the lizard sounds like a lot more fun than the executive.

Obviously, all of this is an oversimplification of how the brain works, something we're only now, through advanced technologies, getting a scientific feel for. However, for our purposes, the above descriptions and nicknames will be sufficient and helpful.

Using functional magnetic resonance imaging (fMRI) machines, neuroscientists have recently developed proof that "delaying delayed gratification" is biologically quite natural. By tracking which parts of our brain are activated when we're forced to choose between immediate and future rewards (like consuming now or saving), we can better understand our decision-making processes.

In a variety of studies, the results are similar. Both rewards — the instantaneous and the delayed — create activity in our prefrontal cortexes (our executives), but the immediate rewards also cause significant activity in our limbic system. They awaken our lizards!

Remember, these emotion-driven reptiles thrive on pleasure in the here and now.

Uh-oh.

According to the neuroscientists, we can blame this on our prehistoric ancestors. Their brains developed to deal with the challenges of a different time, such as dodging a sabre-toothed tiger or running away from a suitor wielding a club. Immediate needs and threats dominated their every thought. Building an RRSP seldom crossed their minds.

The problem is that the "equipment" for the old times isn't very well suited to the complexities of our new life. Sure, evolution has provided us with a growing ability to process information and to reason — our executive has matured nicely. Unfortunately, though, millions of years later, especially when faced with an immediately accessible temptation, our decisions still echo those of our cavemen and cavewomen forerunners — "I want it and I want it now." In essence, our brain is wired so that if the emotional excitement created by the temptation is high enough, whether it's a second piece of cake or the newest high-tech gizmo, it can overwhelm our good senses and make us discount, or even forget, our best-laid plans.

Oscar Wilde's self-assessment, "I can resist everything except temptation," leaps to mind.

Perhaps the answer, argue some neuroeconomists (and all grandmas), is not to try to resist temptation, but to avoid it altogether. They recommend, especially if we have a predisposed weakness to a certain temptation, not to get close enough to it that our senses can engage with it. Once our sight, smell and touch connect to desirable objects, both formal research and our own frequent failings show that we're in trouble. Our dopaminergic neurons get excited and our lizards get all fired up — maybe even wild(e).

I can relate. I exercise discipline and eat healthfully for weeks on end, but put me in a mall food court with an A&W and all hell breaks loose. The sweat dripping down the outside of the frosted mugs…the smell of bacon and fries…even the orange and brown uniforms…it's all too much for me. Two Teen Burgers later, I'm wondering how it all went so very, very wrong.

For the longest time, Greta Podleski (one of the *Looneyspoons* cookbook sisters) battled an addiction to buying clothes. She had no self-control (but a lot of gorgeous outfits!). Then suddenly it changed — she mastered her sartorial spending.

"How did you pull that off?" I asked, astounded.

"I stopped visiting clothing stores," was her simple, shrugged response. Hey, I've always said that the best financial strategies are straightforward. Interestingly, when I suggested Greta apply the same approach to her shoe fetish, she replied, "Mind your own business," and continued her discerning shopping style of "If the shoe fits, buy it."

Even though I agree that the neuroeconomists' (and Greta's) avoid-temptation advice is sound, let's be honest, it's not always easy to do. We're all forced to shop from time to time. And, hey, there's tons of incredible stuff out there — it's fun to check it out. Plus, marketers and store designers are reading the new brain research, too. Their devious minds are constantly dreaming up ingenious ways of appealing to our senses and feeding our lizards.

So, we're not wired to resist temptation. That, we know. Avoiding temptation isn't always possible. That, we know. What's left? Simple. Take away the ability to give in to temptation. That's the key!

About a decade ago, I heard a woman being interviewed on an American radio show. She explained that she kept her credit cards in a big block of ice in the freezer. When she came across some item that she "just had to have," she would race home and thaw out the cards, a process that took about a day. Not surprisingly, by then her emotions had cooled and her executive was back in charge. In almost every instance, she decided that she didn't need or even want the product after all. The show's host, a financial planner, thought this rather unusual approach was a bit wacky.

I think it's brilliant. I'm amazed that more people don't force fiscal discipline upon themselves by limiting their access to money and credit. C'mon, you don't think the growing popularity of debit and credit cards and ATM machines has anything to do with our declining savings rates? It's way too easy to overspend now. Giving in to temptation is only a mindless swipe away. Instead of looking into our wallets and spotting a finite amount of cash — the ultimate forced discipline — we see virtually unlimited funds. Why, for heaven's sake, do many average-income Canadians carry $15,000 to $25,000 credit-card limits? It's an invitation to disaster. (And please don't tell me it's for the travel points — flights "earned" through excessive credit-card use are akin to the "free" hotel rooms Vegas offers to heavy gamblers.)

By the way, before you conclude that I'm as wacky as the "ice lady," you should know that neuroeconomists (a.k.a. geniuses) are on our side. They're now urging us to "inject time between the stimulus and response," borrowing from Stephen R. Covey's *The 7 Habits of Highly Effective People.* And the best way to do that? Make it a hassle to get at your money and credit, of course. They haven't advocated the "freeze your spending" idea yet, but they're totally on board with leaving the debit and credit cards at home on occasion, if not regularly. In fact, an idea they've proposed is to own only two credit cards. One you keep at home, with a higher limit for when it's truly needed, such as booking a trip. The other, with a much lower limit, you keep in your wallet for more conventional, everyday use. (Please don't take the expression "everyday use" literally!)

Perhaps someday we can all be Spock-like and not so subject to our emotions. We'll figure out a way to tame our lizards. In the meantime, let's hope scientists develop a little blue pill to cure our "reptile dysfunction."

Infatuation

EVEN WHEN OUR EMOTIONS don't overwhelm our reason, they can still trick it into making bad judgment calls.

Imagine you're at a popular patio bar on a steamy, hot day. You're dying for an ice-cold beer and would happily part with $6 to get a bottle. Your server informs you that your favourite brand is on special for $4.

You, being a normal person (I assume), would probably respond, "Wow, what a fantastic deal! How much are the wings?"

An economist, on the other hand, would probably respond, "Hmm...a consumer surplus of $2 — most interesting." Not surprisingly, few economists thrive in social settings.

The microeconomic term "consumer surplus" means the difference between the price a consumer is willing to pay for something and the price he or she actually pays for it (in other words, its cost). The bigger the consumer surplus, the bigger the bargain. We love bargains! None of this is too deep, I'll concede, but stick with me.

The price we're willing to pay is based on our assessment of how much value the item will bring to our lives. For something we're going to consume immediately, it's a pretty easy evaluation. A pack of Nibs at my local convenience store goes for $1.50. I know, from vast experience, that I'll get at least $5 worth of pleasure from eating those tiny nuggets of black licorice. Nature's food. Dancing taste buds, a joyous heart and a $3.50 consumer surplus — the decision makes itself.

The problem arises when we have to make the value assessment on products we'll use over an extended time frame, such as a new car. Those first few months of quality time with your latest indulgence are worth a lot of "joy units." However, will you still be as excited in three years when your chariot is showing its age? Probably not.

The greater our exposure, the less we're enthralled. That's human nature. Repetition trumps wonderfulness — our possessions yield less pleasure each time we use them. Economists call this declining marginal utility. Psychologists call it habituation. Wives call it husbands.

Consumers, amazingly, don't call it anything. In fact, we usually give no thought whatsoever to declining marginal utility when we're contemplating buying something. Despite thousands of personal experiences to the contrary, we assume that our affection will never wane. The product will somehow always provide us with the pride and joy we're feeling at the time of purchase. Neuroeconomists' research suggests that this flawed and unrealistic anticipation occurs because when our emotions are involved, our wiring leads us to project our immediate feelings into the future. Our "executive's" voice of experience is silenced.

Essentially, it's infatuation and, like its romantic cousin, it also wears off. At the spending-decision time, passion is running hot and logic is running cold. Or away. We extend our excitement forward and thereby overestimate the amount of joy the purchase will give us. The price we are willing to pay is therefore too high, creating bargains in our mind that often never materialize.

Let's be honest, we've all bought things that had us scratching our heads just a few months later. Exercise equipment, anyone?

Lord Byron captured this dilemma well: "The lovely toy so fiercely sought hath lost its charm by being caught." Admittedly, being a poet in the 1800s, Lord Byron was probably referring to a woman and not an espresso machine or a sand wedge. (By the way, I'm no relationship expert, but calling his "catch" a "toy" probably had something to do with her scaling back the charm.)

So, the next time you're tempted to make a major purchase, especially an impulsive one, step back, think a year or two out, and then ask yourself, "Will I still be as pumped as I am right now?"

If you're like most people, you'll answer, "Absolutely!"

Oh well, I tried.

Choose Your Friends Wisely

EVERYTHING IN LIFE IS RELATIVE. I'm short compared to Shaq, yet tall compared to my daughter. I'm old compared to a baby, but young up against my dad. I'm a dunce compared to Einstein, yet fairly clever compared to most house pets.

How we feel about our possessions and lifestyles is also relative. Relative to what? To the possessions and lifestyles of our friends and colleagues, of course.

Sadly, we often can't appreciate what we have for its own merit. Instead, we only consider ourselves fortunate when we have as much as (or even better, more than!) those with whom we most closely identify.

We compare. We covet. We consume.

Ivan Illich, the Austrian philosopher, noted decades ago that in a consumer-driven society we act like slaves, prisoners of envy.

Some envy is quite natural. Its evolutionary roots developed at a time when resources, including that all-important one — food — were truly scarce. Life was a competition with survival as the prize. We were, therefore, wired millenniums ago to want what others have. And that's OK when the others fall within our general earnings category. It's not so OK when they make three times what we do.

When Harvard economist James Duesenberry penned his classic 1949 paper on "keeping up with the Joneses," the featured family was middle class and lived within their means. Yes, their neighbours, who probably also doubled as their close friends, wanted to be like the Joneses and keep up by owning the same car and appliances, but that was fine. They *were* like the Joneses! Their incomes were similar.

Nowadays, friendships are less likely to be grounded in the neighbourhood. Instead, they tend to develop at the workplace, the gym, the children's sporting venues and even online. That's great, but it regularly exposes us to the spending habits of people across a much wider income range, including the modern-day, more affluent Joneses. We hitch rides in their fancy cars. We marvel at their exotic vacations. We are in awe of their sons' new $500 hockey sticks. We soak in Facebook photos of their spectacular cottages.

It's hard to overstate the impact our "reference groups" have on our spending decisions. We consciously and unconsciously take in their consumption cues. Their lifestyles intoxicate us and when partnered with the great enabler — easy credit — lead us to act richer than we are, "act" obviously being the key word.

What's the solution? Well, one idea advanced by Quentin Crisp, the flamboyant British writer and raconteur, is, "Never keep up with the Joneses. Drag them down to your level. It's cheaper." Sage advice, to be sure, but tough to implement. Hauling your wealthier friends, kicking and screaming, into the local greasy spoon doesn't exactly make for a relaxing night out.

Instead, many experts push us to ignore the Joneses altogether, and do our best to hang out only with people who make the same amount of money as we do. From a purely financial-planning perspective, that would be a wise move, indeed. Realistically, though, asking for people's T4s before forming a friendship seems somewhat inappropriate.

Interestingly, there is a subset of people for whom this like-reference-group selection happens quite naturally: teachers. Thomas J. Stanley, PhD, the author of the mega-selling *The Millionaire Next Door*, has long argued that the fact that teachers work only with people of similar incomes — other teachers — is one of the key reasons that, for the most part, they are so adept at living within their means. His extensive research continuously places educators near or at the top of the financially responsible pile. He's definitely on to something. If anything, he understates his case. Teachers not only work with other teachers, but also form a disproportionate percentage of their friendships within their profession. Makes sense — they share holidays and work schedules and, given the nature of their jobs, tend to be outgoing, social people. Heck, a lot of teachers even marry fellow teachers (an inbreeding I'm not entirely comfortable with).

So, there you have it. The key to controlling your spending is to either gain access to your prospective friends' tax filings or become a teacher. How's that for practical, life-changing advice? Aren't you glad you bought this book?

Kidding aside, this reference-group problem is a big one. In fact, many of the best minds in sociology, including Juliet Schor, author of the oft-quoted *The Overspent American*, think it might be the single biggest cause of our plunging savings rates. They're probably right, in that the weaknesses examined in the chapters "Consumed With Consumption" and "Status Update" flow directly from our obsession with keeping up.

Much of what society deems conspicuous consumption is really competitive consumption.

Again, though, the experts' traditional advice to choose your friends by their incomes is obviously impractical. But there are approaches presented in the next two chapters that have proven to make a big difference, yet are seldom discussed.

The Power of Perspective

SO, WE'RE TOLD THAT OUR APPETITE for more stuff is being whetted by our expanding reference groups. The lifestyles of more prosperous friends, colleagues and even "TV acquaintances" form the vortex of excessive spending. Experts counsel us to shrink our reference groups, when at all possible, to include only those who share our financial profile.

I couldn't disagree more. In fact, I advise you to do exactly the opposite: Expand your reference group as much as possible.

Look around the world. Include everyone.

There is no more potent antidote for the disease of envy than a dose of perspective.

Have you seen what's happening in North Africa? Haiti? Rural China?

From extreme poverty to military rule to the institutionalized abuse of women to non-existent health care — the problems that billions of our world's citizens face daily should shine a light on just how fortunate we are. Note the word "should." Somehow, though, we've lost perspective and seem oblivious to the most important of facts: As Canadians, we won the country-of-residence lottery. We live in a prosperous, democratic, peaceful and beautiful nation. Our lives, by all but one standard, are incredibly rich. Sadly, that one standard — the opulent lifestyles of the very few who have more than we do — is often the only one on which we focus.

Bluntly, too often we treat the non-possession of what most of the world would consider an extreme-luxury item as an unjust deprivation.

Is it really that big a deal that your friend at work has a 32-jet, six-person hot tub and you don't? Nine hundred million people across the globe don't have ongoing access to safe drinking water.

Frustrated that you can't locate a high-speed wireless connection? Remind yourself that more than a billion people don't have electricity.

Annoyed that you don't have stainless-steel appliances? Keep in mind that one in six people in the world goes to bed hungry every night.

Our pets live more comfortably than half the Earth's population, for heaven's sake.

We obsess so much about what we don't have that it affects our ability to enjoy what we do have.

At a luncheon where I was speaking recently, one of the men seated at my table was nearly apoplectic because the TVs in his new, state-of-the-art SUV weren't high definition. What do you say to something like that? Perhaps we should divert international aid to address the problem so that he and his family won't have to suffer any longer.

We should expand our reference groups not only to include the less fortunate throughout the world, but also to encompass those who have gone before us.

Many Canadians are completely out of touch with how much our lives have improved over time. These *are* "the good old days"! It drives me crazy that people can't see that. Even the most optimistic economist of the 1970s, Julian Simon, didn't forecast the incredible bounty that has come our way. We're livin' the dream, as the kids say.

Let's look at a few quick examples, starting with our grocery stores. Amazing foods from all over the world are now at our fingertips. Nothing, not even berries, ever seems to be out of season. The selection in every aisle is nuts — including nuts themselves. In the peanut category alone, you can choose from salted, unsalted, roasted, dry-roasted, unroasted, butter-roasted, honey-roasted, shelled, unshelled, sugar-coated, yogurt-coated, chocolate-coated, hot 'n' spicy, bold 'n' zesty, smoky hickory, jalapeño-scented, barbecue, garlic and chili, and, believe it or not, the list goes on. How spoiled are we? Frozen entrées actually taste like real food now (remember the original Salisbury steak?). Salads come prewashed and ready to serve. We can buy fresh lobster in my landlocked hometown, Kitchener-Waterloo. Insane. Yet, somehow, food costs (as a percentage of our incomes) have trended down over the last century. Better quality. Higher safety standards. More variety. Healthy alternatives. Lower costs. Wow, there must be something to gripe about. Oh, that's right — my store still doesn't stock that thin-crust, multi-grain, low-sodium, nut-free, organic barbecue-chicken pizza that I tasted last week at my sister's place. How will I survive?

What about cars? They're unbelievable nowadays. Tires almost never go flat and when they do, some can re-inflate themselves. Who comes up with this stuff? You can buy cars now that will even parallel park on their own. Yes, on their own! Sign me up — I won't have to hold up traffic for 20 minutes anymore. Air bags. Better fuel efficiency. Anti-lock brakes. Power everything. High-end stereos. Navigation systems. Are you kidding me? Still not enough for some, though. I complimented a friend on how cool his heated seats were (so to speak) and he responded, "I guess, but I really wish I had a heated steering wheel." Hey, tough it out, big fella.

TVs? What can you say? High definition. Large, plasma screens. Hundreds of channels. There's a channel specifically for golf. For food. For the stock market. For the Leafs. The Leafs? And what about the remote? Man, what an ace invention. Have you ever been in a hotel room and your remote doesn't work? You go into complete and utter shock and just keep pointing, pressing and panicking. Move five feet to change channels? That's crazy talk! Think of TVs 40 years ago. Many were still black and white. We got three channels: CBC, CTV and the same CBC broadcast but from another tower. Heck, the dial only had 13 options on it and Channel 1 was UHF. I know now that UHF stands for Ultra High Frequency, but when I was a kid I assumed it meant Unbelievably Hard to Focus. The reception, even on the "good" channels, seemed to go snowy every time Mannix or Ironside was about to catch the bad guy. We'd force Mom to adjust the bunny ears with a metal coat hanger in her mouth — hey, whatever it took. Now people lose it when their PVR misses taping the first 30 seconds of *American Idol*. The tragedy of it all.

How about phones? When I was a kid, we had a rotary phone. It took six minutes to dial someone. Plus, it seemed like everybody's number ended in a zero. If your finger slipped on that all-but-impossible loop to glory, you had to start the whole process over. Long distance was so expensive, it was viewed as a special treat. When friends flew to a vacation down south, which was a very rare occurrence, we'd all be nervous about the safety of the "metal birds." To let us know they had arrived unharmed, our pals would call us at a predetermined time, let the phone ring twice and then hang up. "Woohoo! Tom and Mary made it!" we'd yell in celebration. How silly does that seem now? Plan B was even more hysterical. Tom would call collect and have the operator ask for Gertrude. "Sorry, wrong number," we'd deceitfully reply, as thrilled about outsmarting Ma Bell as by our friends' safe arrival. Party lines? Pay phones? Calling cards? They all seem antiquated in these days of phones that are smarter than we are. Almost everyone now carries a powerful minicomputer that allows him or her to reach anybody, anywhere, anytime at a reasonably low cost. These dynamic devices also often serve as cameras, daily planners, jukeboxes, video-game consoles and Internet portals and run a bunch of apps that I'll never understand. We have the world in the palms of our hands — literally.

Think about all of this. Don't take it for granted. It's mind-boggling but true that the average Canadian lives a much better life than did the kings and queens of wealthy empires just decades ago. That's decades, not centuries.

Harold Coffin, the late Associated Press columnist, noted: "Envy is the art of counting the other fellow's blessings instead of your own." It sounds corny, but most of the people I've known who are adept at living within their means don't make that mistake. They have perspective and fully grasp how lucky they are to be right here, right now. From that knowledge flows gratitude. Obviously, people who are truly thankful for what they do have are less likely to focus on what they don't have. That goes a long way toward controlling spending.

Cicero had some great thoughts on the importance of gratitude and perspective, yet the most insightful line on the subject comes not from the Roman philosopher, but from one of my mom's favourites, 1950s actress and singer Doris Day: "Gratitude is riches. Complaint is poverty."

That's my all-time favourite financial quote.

Four Liberating Words

MARK QUINN, A LONG-TIME FRIEND of mine, called me about a year ago with one of the most common financial-planning problems. "I'm spending too much," he admitted, "and could really use your advice."

I dropped by his office the next day and pressed him for more details. "It's simple, really," he explained. "Every time someone asks me to golf or go out for dinner or take in a hockey game, I say yes. It's getting ridiculous — my lifestyle isn't matched to my income. I've gotta cut back. Can you help me? What are some techniques?"

"Well," I instructed him, "sometimes when people ask you to do something, you'll have to reply, 'I can't afford it.'"

"That's it?" he replied incredulously. "That's all I get? What about a budget? Or cutting up my credit cards? Or one of your boring lectures on the psychology of spending? Something? Anything?"

"Just try it," I pushed him.

"Man, I can't believe you're a bestselling financial author... whatever," was his unusual thank you.

A month later, I phoned Mark and asked if he wanted to grab a bite to eat and get caught up.

"I can't afford it," he replied with a laugh. "Seriously, you won't believe what a difference saying that has made. I've cut back on my spending and I don't feel any pressure to always go along. I'm less stressed — it's all good. It sounds crazy, but I actually *like* saying it."

Paradoxically, "I can't afford it" is not a limiting statement, but a liberating one. It frees you from the pressures to live beyond your means, and its unassailable truth makes it easier to deal with temptation. The fact is, we all have finite resources. We can't possibly do and buy everything we want. There's no shame in that. Accept it. Don't fight it. And don't let your credit cards convince you otherwise.

"I can't afford it." It sounds dramatic, but remembering to use those four simple words on occasion will do a lot more for your financial future than hundreds of hours spent researching mutual funds or developing an intricate budget.

~

Wow. I'll admit it sounds odd to say this about my own advice, but I can't believe the impact the above lesson has had on my test readers. It's been fascinating — person after person ultimately has had the same response as Mark.

For example, Sherri Amos, my liaison when I speak for Home Hardware, happened to call me right after I finished writing this chapter. I read it to her over the phone to see what she thought. Frankly, if she enjoyed it, she hid her enthusiasm well. But two weeks later, she called back and passed on the following story: "Yesterday, my husband and I were about to book our flights to Florida for a family vacation and we felt very stressed. Four kids and we're travelling over March break — you can imagine how expensive the tickets are. It's nuts. Then I remembered our conversation and blurted out, 'We can't afford it! Let's drive!' It felt fantastic — like a weight off our shoulders. We accepted that it was way too expensive to fly and now we're totally charged up about the trip! Unbelievably, you were right!"

Why is it so unbelievable that I was right?

To be honest, I expected there would be not just some resistance but possibly huge resistance to this idea because of pride issues, especially when readers were dealing with their friends. That hasn't been the case. In fact, it seems to have created a sense of relief among those who've used it. It's almost as though people have been waiting for permission to "just say no." And once they begin to respond "I can't afford it" on occasion, they quickly realize that it's not an admission of failure — it's an acceptance of reality and no big deal. Their spouses don't leave them. Their friends still call. Their retirement plans thank them.

Their kids, on the other hand, yell, "Everybody else has one!" and slam doors but, hey, you can't please everyone.

Ditto Diderot

ONE OF THE FINEST PIECES EVER written on the saving-versus-spending challenge was an essay penned way back in 1772 by the witty and wise French philosopher Denis Diderot. It was titled, "Regrets on Parting With My Old Dressing Gown: Or, A Warning to Those Who Have More Taste Than Money."

In it, Diderot eloquently chronicles how his beautiful, new, scarlet dressing gown came to wreak havoc on both his mood and his finances. Soon after receiving the gown, it became apparent that his surroundings, though formerly very pleasing to him, were not in keeping with the gown's elegance. He felt compelled to replace his tapestry, his artworks, his bookshelves and chairs and, finally, even his beloved table that had served as his desk. Eventually, a poorer Diderot sat uncomfortably in his stylish and now formal study. "I was absolute master of my old dressing gown, but I have become a slave to my new one," he lamented.

All of us have some Diderot in us. Therefore, the reference "group" you often need to be most wary of is not your affluent friends, or even your wealthier work colleagues; it's you, yourself.

Few things influence your spending decisions of today more than your spending decisions of yesterday.

Spending begets spending.

The aforementioned cookbook author and entrepreneur Greta Podleski provides us with a perfect example. Not surprisingly, it involves clothing. Several years ago, "GP" informed me that she had just bought a stunning dress at a "ridiculously" low price. "I couldn't afford *not* to buy it!" was her interesting assessment.

If the story stopped there, it wouldn't have been that big a deal. But, of course, it didn't. Defying all mathematical odds, none of Greta's 90-plus pairs of shoes was a match to her version of Diderot's gown. That problem was solved $140 later. However, a new one had taken its place. Astonishingly, not one of GP's purses from her vast collection was "a suitable partner" to the new shoes. The colours clashed or — "wouldn't you know it" — the bronze clasp didn't perfectly complement the copper hue of her newly purchased footwear.

"I need a new purse or the rest of the money I've spent will be wasted," Greta reasoned.

"You can't afford *not* to buy a purse," I replied.

"Exactly," she agreed, apparently immune to sarcasm.

Two tubes of lipstick and a pair of earrings later, *The Curious Case of the Inexpensive Dress That Wasn't* came to a close.

I probably shouldn't throw stones here. Last year, I bought two new fairway woods to hit from the rough, ironically. Suddenly, with my new woods beaming from my bag, my irons looked old and tired to me, as I'm sure I did to them. Once they had been replaced, it was only fitting to add a fantastic high-tech driver and a properly weighted-for-my-stroke putter. Carrying all this new equipment quickly made my previously attractive golf bag appear ratty, tatty and not so natty. So I replaced it, too, followed a few days later by the purchase of a deluxe pair of golf shoes that seemed to boast almost superhuman powers. Eighteen hundred dollars poorer, I had the look of a professional.

My swing, though, showed great resistance, warded off the ghost of Diderot and refused to join the rush to "new and improved." It remained a unique cross between those of Jim Furyk and Lizzie Borden. I hate golf.

Nowhere does the "Diderot effect" do more financial harm than in the area of home renovations. In fact, I'm convinced that during the renovation process, many people go temporarily insane — well, for most it's temporary. How else can their spending decisions be explained? First, most set their initial budgets from slightly to wildly beyond what their finances and common sense would dictate. Then, invariably, the projects come in over budget because, well, that's what projects do. "If we're going to redo the bathroom floor, we might as well put in radiant heating while the tile is pulled up." Finally, and most troublingly, once the bathroom has become palatial, the kitchen pales by comparison. "Our cupboards are so 2000." Diderot is once again resurrected and the "cycle of renovation" rolls on.

The four most expensive words in the English language? "While we're at it…." And the four most expensive letters? HGTV.

I'm not saying "Never renovate." Heck, a lot of my close friends and family members are in the industry and I made significant improvements to my own home a couple of years ago. I love Mike Holmes. But, for crying out loud, get a hold of yourself or, as I wish someone would have advised me as I Dideroted my way down the fairway: Get a grip! The upgrades, including the future changes that the current reno will inevitably lead to, have to be completed within the context of affordability.

More than half of the people I know who are in trouble with their lines of credit (more on that to come) arrived there via excessive home-renovation expenses. I really don't have a problem with indulgences like heated marble floors — I wish I had them. However, when people are purchasing that type of opulent item, especially with borrowed money, while not fully funding their RRSPs or saving for their children's educations, yeah, that's an issue. And, in this particular case, there's no excuse: The low-cost, old-style technology still works wonderfully — buy slippers!

Remember Diderot. Above all, remember the alternative title of his insightful piece: "A Warning to Those Who Have More Taste Than Money."

Plastic Surgery

I FEAR CREDIT CARDS. I REALLY DO. You would be hard pressed to find a financial writer who doesn't. They're potentially evil (not financial writers, credit cards). Before you counter, "Hey, that's a little strong," here are the dictionary definitions of evil: (1) causing ruin, injury or pain; (2) characterized by or indicating future misfortune.

See what I mean?

Some people, especially and not coincidentally bankers, will argue, "Yes, credit cards have put many Canadians into financial trouble, but they offer great convenience."

Well, they're off by a single word. The accurate statement? "Yes, credit cards have put many Canadians into financial trouble *because* they offer great convenience."

Making it easier to do something bad — in this case, to overspend — is not a positive.

Remember, so far we've looked at reason after reason as to why we're so drawn to consumption. We're wired to spend — literally and figuratively. Resisting temptation has always been difficult, but with a wallet full of credit cards, it's darn near impossible.

See. Salivate. Swipe.

Rationalize. Rinse. Repeat.

Amazingly, the spending pattern that results in so many of us getting in over our heads is that basic. As we discussed in the chapter "Faulty Wiring," credit cards allow us to act impulsively on our impulses. (That's not redundant — honest!)

As troubling, they also help *create* those impulses by making us less sensitive to cost. Brain scans show that we react to spending decisions the same way we react to actual physical pain. The part of our limbic system associated with pain recognition (the insula) is triggered when we see the price of an item. In essence, that sends a signal that we may be about to sustain or worsen an injury (of the financial type, in this case). It literally hurts to think of parting with something we value — money. That's a positive in that the painful feeling of prospective loss can counterbalance the emotional excitement we so often feel when contemplating a purchase. The pain is a warning to think before acting.

However, credit cards disrupt this process. As George Loewenstein, a neuroeconomist at Carnegie Mellon University, points out, they "anesthetise the pain."

He explains, "Unlike cash, where you are turning something over (bills and coins) as you are receiving something (a good or service), with credit cards you or the store clerk simply swipes the card, which doesn't feel like giving something up. With credit cards it is also easier to miss, or deliberately ignore, how much one is spending."

Amen.

Often, you hear financial experts say, "For some, credit cards are an issue. However, for those who don't carry a balance, they offer an interest-free loan and are an excellent tool." That last point isn't necessarily true. Even among those who fully pay off their cards each month, many still overspend. They may not charge so much that they're forced to roll over balances, but they do spend enough to block themselves from saving the appropriate amounts. They, too, have a credit-card "issue."

It's really this simple: Credit cards allow us to act wealthier than we are and acting wealthy now makes it tough to be wealthy later.

Here's the real stinger. I've warned about credit cards for a couple of pages already and haven't even mentioned their most obvious weakness: They charge absurdly high interest rates on unpaid balances. Obviously, making minimum monthly payments and carrying your debt at 18 percent (or higher) is not a recommended financial-planning strategy.

So, what to do? Realistically, we're not about to cut up our cards. But here's an idea that could jolt us back to reality.

Many times after studying someone's finances (particularly someone in his or her 20s or 30s), I've thought it would be great if swiping a credit card would send a huge electric shock through the spender's body — nothing life-threatening, of course, but enough to get his or her attention. This would give the term "charge it" a whole new meaning! It would certainly make people think twice before recklessly pulling out their plastic. Strangely, the banks and retailers don't seem too keen on my idea.

More practically, we need to expand on the advice given in "Faulty Wiring" about limiting our access to credit. Recognize that charge cards are the great enabler of our addiction to spending, and don't always carry one with you. You *can* leave home without it! Use your debit card to withdraw cash. Remember cash? Paper stuff and some metal? Feel the pain when you pay. Determine a reasonable budget ahead of your shopping excursions and force yourself to stick to it by taking only that amount in *real* money. Don't take your credit card. Don't take your debit card. Take cash — the forgotten currency!

A few years ago, I went to Las Vegas with eight women (don't ask). One of them employed this simple strategy before heading to the malls: She would withdraw a reasonable amount from an ATM, then leave all her cards in the hotel room's safe. Not only did it work like a charm, but she claimed it also reduced her stress while "hunting" because it forced her to be a more discerning shopper. All good.

When my sister and brother-in-law were first married, one of them had a problem with over-the-top spending. Obviously, it would be highly inappropriate to specify which one. (It was my sister!) So, they moved to more of a cash-based system, cut her plastic down to one credit card and lowered its limit. Problem solved; they've never looked back. Plus — and this is a key point — my sister swears she's no longer tempted to overspend because, well, she can't.

A final approach worth considering is, I'll admit, a bit out of the ordinary. Over the years, I've had a lot of success helping people gain control over their credit-card spending simply by sternly lecturing them. Nothing more. Seriously. I'm not sure why an old-fashioned tongue-lashing has proven so effective in dealing with this particular dilemma. I normally believe in an upbeat, encouraging approach. One "cured" woman's theory was that I reintroduced the spending-decision pain, in that every time she went to use her card, my harsh words echoed in her mind. Hey, whatever works. So, if you find yourself overusing your credit cards, call my office at (519) 747-2298 and I'll yell at you for a few minutes — no charge. Pardon the pun.

Perhaps you're one of the few people with the self-discipline to avoid the pitfalls of credit cards. You love the travel points and the extended warranties on purchases. Even if that's the case, stay vigilant — their charms can lure almost everyone in eventually.

Evil lurks.

Taking Too Much Credit

LINES OF CREDIT FASCINATE ME. While normal folks enjoy watching their favourite TV shows, hitting the theatre for a new blockbuster or reading a bestselling novel, I like studying how and why people take on debt.

No wonder I live alone. Pathetic.

That admission aside, lines of credit (LOCs), and the way Canadians have embraced them, really are interesting. Some experts describe them as "very helpful." Others label them "insidious." How can they be both?

Well, let's start at the beginning — what exactly is an LOC? It's a pretty basic concept, actually. It's an arrangement where a financial institution agrees to lend money up to a specified limit to a customer. Borrowers can use as much, or as little, of the available amount as they want, when they want. What's more, there aren't usually any rules that dictate how the funds must be deployed. Plus, with the majority of LOCs, the repayment schedules are non-existent. Clients can pay back the money "whenever" and, in many instances, make interest-only payments each month. For consumers, this keeps the loans' servicing costs way down. Finally, most LOCs, because they're secured by the borrowers' home equity, offer very competitive interest rates.

What's not to like? All of these features make lines of credit very flexible and give almost complete control to the customers.

Therein lies the problem.

In essence, lines of credit are like giant credit cards but with much lower interest rates and no travel points. And like their plastic cousins, LOCs allow us to mindlessly give in to temptation and live beyond our means.

In the hands of responsible, disciplined and thoughtful borrowers, a credit line can be an excellent financial tool. The other 71.9 percent of Canadians, however, should be careful. Very careful.

People have gone wild with these things over the last two decades. Can't afford something? No worries, just "throw it on the line of credit." I have friends who treat their LOCs like a second income. Others, when they first set up their lines of credit, spend as if they've won the lottery.

Even some of my financially responsible colleagues have built up huge balances on their credit lines, half the time without fully realizing it was happening. Hence the earlier descriptive, "insidious" — beguiling but harmful, intended to entrap.

It's not hard to see why so many Canadians have fallen under the spell of lines of credit. The combination of interest-only monthly payments and all-time-low borrowing rates has made credit lines seem almost like free money.

Last year, I was helping a woman who had some financial questions and she mentioned that she had borrowed $60,000 against her LOC to renovate her sons' bathrooms. (Yeah, I know what you're thinking.) "Don't worry about that," she assured me. "The reno only costs me $150 a month. I can afford it."

Only $150 a month? That can't be right, can it? Her LOC's rate was three percent and three percent of $60,000 is $1,800 a year or $150 a month. That's only $5 a day.

While doing that math, the thought, "Hey, I want a line of credit for $60,000, too," danced through my head. Man, these things really are beguiling — they're sucking me in even as I write a piece warning against them. I'm like the Crown attorney who falls for the beautiful murderess he's trying to prosecute. OK, that's weak — but, seriously, an LOC is hard to resist.

So why fight it? Well, let's go back to the woman's claim that the reno costs her only $150 a month. Wrong. Very wrong. It costs her $150 a month plus the $60,000!

She conveniently forgot the principal repayment. Her bank, rest assured, will not. She *will* have to pay it back someday. And that's a lotta moolah. Even if she tries to spread the repayment over five years, it will still cost her $1,000 a month in principal payments alone. Discharging the loan won't be easy.

Many borrowers' answer? Don't pay it back, just leave it there indefinitely. Worry about it later…much later…in fact, maybe the ultimate later — at death. Essentially, a good number of Canadians are taking on homemade, quasi reverse mortgages. They're borrowing with a secured line of credit and, sometimes consciously, sometimes unconsciously, planning to pay it back from either the great beyond or when they sell their homes and move to more humble dwellings.

Something tells me this situation isn't going to have a happy ending. The last thing we need is a nation of people carrying significant debt loads into already insufficiently funded retirements.

And what happens if interest rates go up? Or perhaps I should say, what happens *when* interest rates go up? We're not going to be living in an easy-credit environment forever. At 3 percent, all this borrowing is manageable. At 7 percent, it's tough. At 11 percent, buy some canned goods and head for the basement — we're in big trouble.

Those legitimate warnings aside, lines of credit can be a wise choice when financing is needed. I'm not saying that just to sound balanced, either; they really can be.

For example, if you're borrowing to invest, an idea we'll explore later, an LOC can play a helpful role — flexible and efficient.

If you're consolidating or refinancing debt, a line of credit is ideal — flexible and efficient.

Again, though, for those prone to overspending (and that's most of us!), credit lines are a willing accomplice — flexible and efficient.

Their strength is their weakness. They are very helpful, yet insidious. 'Twas the best of products. 'Twas the worst of products.

You get my point. They're a financial paradox.

So exercise extreme caution. And when drawing from your line of credit, always remember this incredibly basic but ultra-important fact: It's not your money, it's your bank's.

All Too Willing to Lend a Hand

LAST YEAR, OUR OFFICE RECEIVED a call from a woman desperate to track me down. As you can guess from my cover photo, that's a rare occurrence, so I got back to her immediately.

She frantically declared that she was "in a bit of a pickle" (her words, not mine). A few years earlier, she had inherited a home from her parents and started to slowly build an RRSP. Unfortunately, by her own admission, she was a shopaholic and was abusing her credit cards. In just two years, she had run up an astounding $30,000 in debt. The good news was that she was fully aware that her interest charges were astronomical and that her lack of fiscal discipline was a threat to her financial future. She sincerely wanted to straighten out her act.

I counselled her to head to her bank's loan department and arrange for a $30,000 secured line of credit — nothing more. Pay off the credit cards with the LOC, thereby refinancing from 18 percent debt to 3 percent debt, and cut up the cards immediately. The plan was to then set up a monthly pre-authorized transfer from her chequing account to chisel away at the loan.

Just one week later, she called back and excitedly confirmed that she had done as instructed. Her cards were paid off in full.

"It felt great," she enthused. "It really did."

"Did you cut up the cards?" I pushed.

"Absolutely!" she exclaimed. "And I won't be tempted to get new ones, either, especially with my $150,000 line of credit."

"What?! I told you to get a $30,000 line of credit...$30,000 and nothing more!"

"I know, but the nice young man said that with my fully paid-for home and income, he felt the $150,000 level was more appropriate. Like he said, it's there if I need it, but I don't have to use it."

"Kind of like your credit cards," I pointed out. "Did you mention to the 'nice young man' that you have a spending problem? That you can't control your shopping desires? That you can't resist the allure of available credit?"

"Yes, and he assured me that's quite common."

Dumbfounded, I wasn't sure how to proceed after that comment so, with her permission, I phoned the loan officer. I asked him, point-blank, why he gave a huge line of credit to a customer who hadn't requested it and who had admitted that she has a significant spending issue.

His answer was succinct, honest and illuminating.

"It's my job," he said.

Banks are a business and, like all businesses, they sell something. In their case, that something is money. (Technically, they're renting it to us, but you get the point.)

At its core, a bank's business model is very straightforward. It borrows money from depositors at X percent (yes, you're loaning the bank funds when you put your paycheque into your account) and then it lends those monies to other parties who need financing at X + Y percent.

The bank's profit before overhead costs is Y percent (known as the net interest margin). That assumes, of course, that none of the borrowers default on their loans. As we've seen over the last few years, though, borrowers have developed a nasty habit of doing just that.

Banks throughout the world have, once again, been reminded of the obvious: Lending money to people who probably can't pay it back is not a great way to grow your business. This is doubly true when the loans' collateral is bubble-priced real estate.

However, Canadian banks, some of the best run and most wisely regulated in the world, have exercised prudence. For the most part, they've avoided lending more and more money to the I'll-be-able-to-make-my-payments-if-everything-goes-perfectly crowd. Instead, they've focused much of their marketing energy on getting the customers who have excellent security (usually in the form of ample home equity) and the wherewithal to service loans to borrow as much as possible, whether they ask for it or not.

It's no longer only about providing credit to those who need it, now it's also about convincing people they should want it. Live your dreams. You deserve it. Buy a winery.

In short, our financial institutions have become aggressive. They're no longer just credit providers. They're credit pushers.

It's key to understand that your bank's metric for debt afford-ability and your metric as the prospective borrower are very different, or at least they should be. All the bank calculates is whether you can make the monthly loan payments, based on your income and other debt servicing. You, on the other hand, need to determine whether you can make all of your loan pay-ments while still funding your retirement programs, perhaps doing some other saving and — not unimportantly — having a life. We'll look at this more closely soon.

Bluntly, your bank's effort to load you up with as much debt as you can service is often not in your best interest. Pun intended.

Am I saying that nobody at your bank cares about your financial future? Of course not. Many do, but they don't normally work in the loan department. Think back to the earlier story. That young loan officer had a true conflict of interest — literally, as he wanted the customer to pay more of it. What was best for the client and what was best for his employer weren't aligned. He went with the paycheque and it's hard to blame him.

I hate blasting the banks. I enjoy working with them and have (or had!) a ton of friends in the industry. Now they may not hire me to speak and I'm not above thinking of my paycheque, either. But for crying out loud, they have got to cool it a bit. We have far too many Canadians carrying more debt than any reasonable analysis would support.

That said, we have to take responsibility for our own decisions. No one can force us to open an LOC with a $200,000 limit or to borrow to our maximum approved mortgage levels (some of which are ridiculous, by the way).

Just say no! You are your own credit-control board.

Let common sense, your savings goals and your financial advisor, not your loan officer, determine your borrowing levels. Factor in human nature; limit your access to money that is not yours.

Too much available credit often leads to too much unaffordable spending. And stress. Lots of stress.

Whoa. The feedback from test readers of this chapter and the previous one has been a great learning experience for me. It's quite apparent that I *understated* the perils of lines of credit. Person after person has recounted horror stories. My "temporary insanity" argument around LOCs and home renovations? Confirmed. It's clear that the battle between "very helpful" and "insidious" is being won by the latter.

Even two loan officers admitted that it's probably worse than I've described. Remember, they make their livings marketing credit lines and they're still saying that! They've seen the damage done, first-hand.

It's interesting that the point that most resonated with readers was, "I have friends who treat their LOCs like a second income." Over and over again, people responded, "Yep, that's us."

"I'm glad our kitchen is so nice; it's just too bad we can't afford food," was one test reader's comment. She was kidding, of course, but her humour reveals an important truth.

Watch your step here! It's clearly often best to throw away the key and not open this type of LOC.

A Borrowed Approach
to Borrowing

I'LL ADMIT THAT I STOLE THIS IDEA. That's not unusual — I steal ideas all the time. What's unusual here is the original source. I didn't pinch this idea from Warren Buffett. Or from Ben Franklin. Or from any other famous financial mind. Nope. I lifted it from an astute woman in Dartmouth, Nova Scotia.

She worked for the government, I believe, and her husband was in manufacturing. Years ago they called me to explain their approach to saving and borrowing and to get my opinion. The wife proudly announced that they used pre-authorized chequing and payroll deductions to fully fund their RRSPs and to do some additional long-term saving. Music to my ears, of course.

The problem was that they had trouble saving for things like a new TV or a trip or a hot tub. The few hundred a month they needed and hoped to set aside constantly slipped through their fingers. They refused to use their credit card and carry a balance (hooray!) and wisely recognized that although a significant line of credit (LOC) would let them finance everything they wanted, that would be an even bigger problem, not a solution.

Their compromise was very clever. They set up a small line of credit of only $7,000 and made a firm promise to each other that once they borrowed, no matter what the amount, they couldn't borrow again until their LOC balance had returned to zero.

Their prudently contained debt (known in the industry as PCD — from now on, anyway) served as the ultimate forced-savings program. They had to pay off their plasma TV if they wanted to go to Mexico. Then they had to pay off the Mexico trip if they wanted new golf clubs. And so on and so on.

Yes, they're giving in to temptation without having the savings, but only one shot at a time and at an affordable level. Their LOC balance never exceeds $7,000 and, once tapped into, it begins a one-way journey back to zero.

What was most interesting was that they loved paying down the debt! The saving that they couldn't manage pre-purchase came easily post-purchase. Why? Their basic strategy had captured the power of materialism and turned it into an incentive. They knew that they could buy something again only when their LOC balance was eliminated.

A strong desire to get back to being debt-free so they could take on more debt (yes, that does sound weird) pushed them to act in a more fiscally responsible way. A unique combination of instant gratification mixed with anticipation worked wonders for them.

More importantly, it's worked equally well for other people to whom I've introduced this concept. They've not only been able to stick to this approach, but they've also enjoyed it. Come to think of it, that's probably why they've been able to stick to it.

I'm guarded with credit lines, yet I like this idea a lot. It's simple — but hey, so am I.

Remember, though, it's a $7,000 line of credit, not a $70,000 line of credit and full repayment is required before another purchase can be financed.

When it comes to a LOC, just don't go LOCO. (My sister came up with that one. She struggles.)

A Story Break

ALL THIS TALK ABOUT SAVING MORE money (or, more depressingly, spending less) can be a bit overwhelming. I thought we'd take a break and I'd share a motivational chapter that has absolutely nothing to do with financial planning. Yes, that's a bit odd but my mom loves this story and I love my mom.

In October 1995, I received a phone call from one Janet Podleski of Ottawa. I'd never heard of her. She rambled on and on about a fantastic, unique cookbook that she and her sister Greta were writing. I couldn't, for the life of me, figure out why she was calling my office. Eventually, I interrupted her.

"I think you have the wrong person. I'm Dave Chilton, the author of *The Wealthy Barber*. I'm a personal-finance guy. I don't know anything about cookbooks or, for that matter, cooking. I'm completely incompetent in the kitchen. Actually, I'm pretty shaky in a couple of other rooms, too. Who are you looking for?"

"You," she insisted. "We read an article about you in *Saturday Night* magazine. It said you had great success self-publishing your book. So we want you to self-publish ours."

I pointed out that logically it would be impossible for me to "self-publish" someone else's work but she wasn't deterred by semantics. She relentlessly forged on. "We'll be a great team," she argued. "You can even be the captain."

"Thanks, but I don't know you and I'm not really a team type of guy. Also, I'm travelling a lot so I have no time for another project. If the book is as amazing as you say, you'll have no problem finding a conventional publishing partner."

"We've been rejected by all 18 we've sent packages to," Janet conceded. "Obviously, they don't know what they're talking about!"

"Obviously," I concurred, admiring her optimism. "Listen, I don't want to waste your time, Janet. I'm not interested, but good luck."

She wouldn't give up and begged me for a meeting. I stuck to my guns and kept saying no. Then, right as I was making my move to hang up, lady luck struck.

"We'll take a train to see you tomorrow," she pleaded as I lowered the phone.

If she hadn't said "train," I never would have agreed. But I thought, "Train? Who takes the train for a quick meeting? People fly. People drive. But the train?" I was intrigued. Plus, and I know this makes me sound like a little kid, I was excited about going to the train station to greet them. I hadn't been there since I was 10. I love trains!

So, the next day, I picked up the persistent Podleskis at the station. Little did I know that that meeting was going to change my life.

They were quite formally attired and one was carrying a laptop — no big deal today, but unusual in 1995. At the restaurant, they launched into a PowerPoint presentation on trends in the health-food industry. I survive on three packs of Nibs a day — the fact that lettuce sales were about to explode was of little interest to me. Truthfully, the entire presentation was painfully boring. I would have devised a way out of there were it not for the fact that we were a perfect match on one front: The sisters are very good looking and I am very shallow.

I hung in, doing my best to feign interest. Finally, I couldn't take it anymore. I leaned over and closed up the laptop. "What happened to yesterday's charisma? Your energy on the phone was incredible. Forget the pie charts and bar graphs. Why are you doing this? What makes you different? Why this book? Tell me your story."

"Well, it all started about 15 months ago," Janet began. "I was working in software sales and bought a new house. Greta needed a place to stay and her rent money would help with the mortgage payments, so she moved into the basement. She's a phenomenal cook — unbelievable, really. She's been cooking since she was seven years old. And I don't mean with an Easy-Bake Oven, either — we're talking full-course meals for our family of eight."

"That *is* impressive," I noted sincerely. "But how did the book idea emerge?"

"Well, Greta started cooking all the dinners at the new house. They were to die for. No more eating out! I would take the left-overs to work the next day for lunch. My co-workers were oohing and aahing over my meals. I was saving a ton of money. Then, after a few months, I noticed I'd lost a few pounds. I felt great — but I was concerned because I hadn't changed my workout regimen at all. I thought maybe I was sick."

"And I told her it was just the opposite," Greta broke in. "I told her she'd been losing weight because of our diet. We'd been eating very nutritious meals — low in fat, better carbs — but she didn't believe me. We'd been eating burgers and pizzas, not bean sprouts and tofu! With creative ingredient substitutions, I just made them much healthier without giving up any taste."

"I knew right then that we had to think big," Janet took over. "The world needed to know about Greta's incredible recipes. We needed to open a restaurant chain called Greta's, from coast to coast. This was going to be huge! Right away, we went to the bank to borrow the money."

"That didn't go well," Greta chimed in. "They wouldn't give us the money because we didn't have a business plan or any capital or any experience or the proper educational backgrounds. That loan officer was tough!"

"Yeah, a real nitpicker," I sympathized. "So then what happened?"

"That's when we decided to write a cookbook!" Greta beamed. "We knew for sure that we were on the right track. I would develop the recipes and Janet would write healthy lifestyle tips in the margins. Then, we'd put our heads together to write corny food jokes to give the book a humorous twist. Everyone loves to eat and everyone loves to laugh...so why not combine the two?"

"So, the very next day, we quit our jobs," Janet announced.

"You what?" I asked in disbelief.

"We quit. On the same day, at the same time. We needed to focus. I walked into my boss's office and said, 'I'm leaving — I'm going home to work on a secret project with my sister!'"

Who talks like that?

"I did the same," nodded Greta. "I was working on Parliament Hill and I walked away from a steady job to join Janet."

"That's crazy! What did you do for money?"

"Oh, it was tough. We had to borrow from boyfriends, ex-boyfriends, cousins, our brother-in-law...whomever. Those funds ran out months ago, though."

"Do you come from a wealthy family?" I wondered.

"No, no," Janet responded. "Our father is deceased and our mother is retired."

"How do you pay your bills?" I demanded, fascinated.

"We don't!" was Janet's shocking reply.

"We don't even open them," Greta shrugged. "We have a drawer — the bill drawer — in the kitchen that we shove them all into. Why would we open them when we can't pay them?"

That question actually made sense to me. The rest of the story? Not so much. "Don't your creditors come after you for payments?" I pressed.

"For sure. The Bell telephone guy was very upset for a while but we told him all about our exciting book project and he's quite supportive now," Greta explained. "Every week, he asks me what recipes I'm working on.

"We owe everybody — it's hard to keep track of it all."

Oh my, this was not something *The Wealthy Barber* author could be party to. In fact, I was getting quite stressed by all of this, which is out of character for me. So much so that I immediately wrote the sisters a cheque for $2,000. I told them, "Someday, if you're successful, you can pay me back." They never did.

At this point, I really wasn't sure what to make of the dynamic duo. On the upside, they had an infectious attitude and loads of personality. On the downside, they were nuts, possibly certifiable.

I held my ground and continued to say no to their partnership overtures.

Janet was like a dog with a bone. "Greta is a genius — an idiot savant. She's like the Rainman of healthy eating. You can give her any meal and, miraculously, she can make it both healthier *and* better tasting. She has no other talents, but this she can do! We've brought along three pieces of her amazing, low-fat cheesecake for you and your office staff to try. If you don't think that it's the best cheesecake you've ever tasted, we'll never bother you again."

"Don't bother me again, regardless," I said, only half-jokingly. I then took the sisters back to the train station, ate all three pieces of the cake (research) and tried to forget the whole encounter.

That proved impossible as Janet and Greta phoned, faxed and emailed me every day. Every time I spoke in Ottawa, there they were in the front row, lip-synching along with me. Media articles later praised their stick-to-itiveness — but really, it was more like stalking.

Finally, there was a breakthrough. After one of my talks, the Podleskis invited me for a coffee and to show me their nearly completed book. It looked great — and very different. Even I, a non-foodie, was drawn to its charm. I decided to take home some sample pages to show my family.

I stopped in at my parents' place to say hello to them after my flight back from Ottawa. While I caught up on the Detroit sports scene (such as it is) with my father, my mother reviewed the sisters' work. She was laughing...a lot. She was also intrigued by the recipes. "These combinations of ingredients are really unusual. Frankly, it doesn't look like they'll work. Interesting."

Then my father, a true linguist, reviewed a few pages. "Who did the editing?" he asked.

"No one yet. That's their copy. How bad is it?"

"It's not. It's excellent. These two have an outstanding command of the English language."

Hmm. "Maybe Janet and Greta are a little sharper than I realized," I remember thinking.

"Mom, do me a favour and whip up a few of the recipes, then let me know what you think, OK?"

One week later, she called and said, verbatim, "That's the best food I've ever made or eaten. You should publish that book."

I speak to a lot of MBA students and I always tell them, "You can do all the focus-group testing you want and all the formal research your heart desires, but when your mom tells you to publish the book, publish the book!"

I phoned Janet's place right away and informed the sisters that I'd had a complete change of heart. "I'm in! I *will* be your partner. I'll bring the capital and the experience; you bring your enthusiasm and the cookbook."

I am not overstating it when I say that they went crazy. I could hear them yelling and screaming, high-fiving, clinking glasses — hysteria. Greta blurted, "OK, we'll come up with a company name tonight and you can incorporate us in the morning! We'll mix our three names together. It'll be great...very clever...promise!"

The next day she called back at 9 a.m. sharp and announced our new company's name: "It's Granet Publishing...*Greta* plus *Janet* equals Granet! Get it?"

"Um, what happened to Dave?" I felt compelled to ask.

"Couldn't get you in there. Sorry!" she chirped.

As you may know or have guessed by now, I'm talking about their book *Looneyspoons*. It launched in September 1996 and went on to set several publishing records, selling a jaw-dropping 850,000 copies in Canada alone in its first 18 months. The industry had never seen anything quite like it.

Janet and Greta's contagious personalities captured the country's attention. Everyone in the media wanted to interview them and share their inspiring story. That exposure gave them some momentum, but then the book's charm and, more importantly, its food took it from there.

The word of mouth spread like wildfire. Everyone was talking about and cooking from *Looneyspoons*.

Not surprisingly, I added absolutely no value and was happy to go along for the ride.

Since then, "The Pod Squad" has released two more bestselling books, *Crazy Plates* and *Eat, Shrink & Be Merry!* They've created a line of healthy frozen-food products, launched greeting cards with Hallmark, designed kitchen utensils and hosted a cooking show on Food Network Canada.

It's a remarkable success story.

I left Janet and Greta's business a few years ago. They finally caught on to what I had known and told them the whole time: They didn't need me.

But what an experience! I'll always owe my mom for getting me involved. Of course, I didn't give her any royalties. I didn't want to demean our relationship with such a crass gesture.

I'll also always owe Janet and Greta. Working with them was a blast, a new adventure every day. They reminded me, through their passion, what business should be all about: helping others. No one cares more about getting Canadians to eat more healthfully than they do. No one.

They also serve as outstanding examples of one of the most underemphasized, yet key, ingredients to success: Be nice! They treat people with kindness and respect at all times. No matter how busy they are, they still find the time to return all of their calls and emails personally.

They're great people. Kinda nuts. But great people.

Owe No!

ALMOST EVERY FINANCIAL-PLANNING book tells us that "good debt" is money borrowed to buy an appreciating asset. "Bad debt," obviously then, is money borrowed to buy a depreciating asset or an experience. Taking on good debt may, over time, help us to increase our net worth. Taking on bad debt, not so much.

The examples typically offered up?

Establishing a mortgage to buy your first house, good debt. Using your credit card to go to Vegas, bad debt.

Getting a student loan to help you attend university, good debt. Tapping your line of credit to purchase fancy outdoor furniture, bad debt.

It's tough to argue with the traditional definitions of "good debt" and "bad debt."

But I'm going to anyway. They don't go far enough. In their current form, they're not fully representative of the way you need to think in order to manage your borrowing decisions wisely.

"Good debt" should be defined as any money borrowed to buy an appreciating asset where the cost of servicing the loan doesn't affect your ability to save to the appropriate level *and* where the principal will be fully repaid before your retirement. "Bad debt" is everything else.

So, do not determine how much debt you can afford based on your gross income, but instead based on your after-tax, after-proper-savings income.

That's truly living within your means.

Just because a cottage is probably an appreciating asset doesn't mean you should borrow ridiculous amounts of money to buy one — even if the bank is willing to "help you out." When your mortgage payments are squeezing out your RRSP contributions, don't kid yourself that you've taken on good debt. You can't spend your dock.

Recently, some financial writers have opined that in select circumstances having some debt in your golden years is acceptable. Man, I could feel my body chemistry change just writing that. "Select" must mean "contrived and extreme." And even then, "acceptable" is not synonymous with "advisable." Survey after survey confirms that retirees with outstanding loans are less happy — even when the payments are easily affordable. Carrying debt is stressful at the best of times, but when you're on a fixed income? Brutal.

And what happens if interest rates shoot up? Do you cut back on your food? Stop golfing? Send the spouse back to work? Pilfer from the kids? (I'll admit the last two ideas don't sound all that bad.)

Don't take debt into retirement! It drains cash flow, creates worry and is subject to interest-rate risks that will most assuredly follow Murphy's Law.

It's intriguing that people who handle their money well instinctively follow this simple approach to borrowing. Yet I don't think I've ever seen it written about or taught in a financial course. Strange. Letting the new definition of "good debt" and "bad debt" govern your credit decisions going forward is crucial to your financial success.

And nowhere is that more true than when buying a home. Taking on too much of conventional wisdom's "good debt" can lead you to being under house arrest.

Under House Arrest

I'VE REALLY BEEN LOOKING FORWARD to writing this chapter, partially because I don't have a very exciting life. But it's more because after 30 years of studying thousands of people's finances, I've come to realize the following piece of advice is absolutely key to achieving your financial goals: Live in a house you can *truly* afford.

Yes, that appears to be self-evident. Yes, it's an extension of the last chapter's lesson. And, yes, it seems like common sense. Regrettably, though, common sense and common practice are not the same thing.

Each year, *The Washington Post* runs its Mensa Invitational contest where readers are asked to add, subtract or change one letter of a word to give it a new meaning. One year's winner was *cashtration*: The act of buying a home, which renders the subject financially impotent for an indefinite period of time.

Very clever. Very poignant. Very envious I didn't come up with it.

A lot of Canadians have been cashtrated and they were their own surgeons, with the banks only too happy to pass the scalpels.

Again, the proper definition of "good debt" is debt: (1) taken on to buy an appreciating asset; (2) where servicing doesn't squeeze out savings; and (3) that will be retired before you are.

The banks' definition of "good debt"? Lent money that will be paid back with interest. That's it. What about our savings? Our retirement deadline? These are not the banks' concerns.

No, the banks' loan officers will not be laying out a comprehensive financial plan for you and saying things like, "In view of your need to set aside $8,000 a year in your RRSP, your appropriate mortgage size is...."

Instead, you'll hear, "In view of your gross family income, your *approved* mortgage size is...."

It's amazing that two words located so closely together in the dictionary, "appropriate" and "approved," can be so far apart when it comes to responsible financial planning.

It's scary, actually.

Recently, I breathlessly ranted to a banker, "It's crazy that if two couples come to see you and they have the same gross family income, you'll qualify them for the same mortgage size even if Mr. and Mrs. A are planning on remaining childless and are members of generous defined-benefit pension plans where they don't even have to make contributions while Mr. and Mrs. B have three kids and no pensions. It's nonsense!"

His response? "Yeah, it really is."

That remark fired me up even more. I had been prepared with a litany of valid points to win the argument, then this guy had the nerve to agree with me. I hate it when that happens.

Darn bankers.

As I said in the last chapter, never borrow based on some formula centred on your pre-tax income. It's your after-tax, after-proper-savings income that matters.

Your savings come first; your borrowing decisions follow. Far too many Canadians reverse the order and get themselves into trouble that's very hard to escape.

What's more, the problem with stretching to the max to buy a house isn't just the oversized mortgage payment. It goes way beyond that.

It's the higher property taxes.

It's the higher utility bills.

It's the higher maintenance costs.

Even more troubling, it's our old friend and your new neighbour — Diderot! Remember, spending begets spending. Nothing affects your spending decisions of today more than your spending decisions of yesterday. And there's no bigger spending decision than how much house to take on.

Stretch to buy your house and you'll inevitably stretch to buy your furnishings, your appliances and even your driveway decorations (i.e., your cars).

Watch out!

Two of the finest minds in personal finance, Charles Farrell (*Your Money Ratios*) and Thomas J. Stanley (*The Millionaire Next Door*) argue that overspending on one's home may be the single biggest inhibitor to achieving financial independence.

The funny thing is that people who live in homes they can truly afford consistently rank very highly in happiness surveys. Perhaps they didn't stretch because they were already content or maybe they were content because they didn't stretch. That cause-and-effect stuff is always tricky. But I suspect it's a combination of both.

Look, I love home ownership, but make sure it's you that owns the home and not the other way around.

By the way, the root of the word "mortgage" is "death pledge."

I'm just sayin'.

My Frustration

YESTERDAY MORNING, I SAT DOWN with *The Wealthy Barber*. It had been so long since I'd read it, much less written it, that it was like seeing it for the first time. I buzzed through it, cover to cover, in a few hours.

This is going to sound ridiculous, but I actually got caught up in the story. I found myself wondering what might have happened to the characters over the years. Do Tom and Cathy hook up? Is Roy still alive? Did Dave stick to the barber's teachings?

I excitedly approached my daughter. "Hey, you want to hear a neat idea? Someday, you should write a sequel to *The Wealthy Barber*. A multi-generational literary project. I've never heard of anything like it. How cool would that be?"

"I've never even read the original, Dad," Courtney yawned. "Can I borrow the car?"

Apparently not that cool.

Anyway, two things really jumped out at me while rereading the book. One, my sister's editing was outstanding. I'm not a very talented writer (as I'm sure you've noticed by now). She overcame a heavy burden while building the characters and refining the dialogue. It's too bad the book's financial lessons somehow escaped her. Two, the early part of Chapter 4, dealing with pay yourself first, was by far the book's most important message.

It's completely inappropriate to say this about my own work, but I love that section. I wouldn't change one word of it, even 20-odd years later. In fact, after being sent literally thousands of financial plans over the last two decades, I'm more convinced than ever that using forced-savings techniques is the single biggest key to achieving one's financial goals.

Save first. Spend the rest. Good.

Spend first. Save the rest. Bad.

It really is that straightforward.

In a strange way, it's unfortunate that such an important concept is so simple. It tends to get trivialized. Viewed as trite. Even dismissed.

Don't make that mistake.

Fighting off all the temptation out there isn't easy. Most of us are weak and as we've seen, it's natural to give in to societal, biological and psychological pressures that lead us to overspend.

Budgeting to save sounds great in theory, but seldom works in practice. Wants turn into needs. Today's concerns overwhelm tomorrow's. "I'll catch up next month" becomes our perennially unfulfilled promise.

Pay yourself first!

Ben Franklin taught it more than 200 years ago using his tremendous wit and wisdom.

Now behavioural economists and brain experts concur it's the way to go.

Formal research and empirical evidence both support it fully.

There's a reason that this concept is in every financial-planning book: It works!

Yet most people don't do it.

I can't tell you how frustrating that is.

Payroll deduction, automatic withdrawal, pre-authorized chequing — I don't care how you do it, just do it!

Not when the basement is finished. Not after the next vacation. Not in a few months when you're hoping to finally have time to craft a financial plan.

Now.

Will you miss the saved money? Will your lifestyle decline? I don't know. Maybe. Sure. But not nearly as much as you'd guess. Honestly. The vast majority of people who institute a forced-savings approach are amazed at how little change they notice in their consumption.

Frankly, even if you do feel a bit of a pinch and have to cut back somewhere, hey, sorry, but you *must* save. I've been studying personal finances my entire adult life and I still haven't discovered a way to set aside some money without, well, setting aside some money.

You know, I've been treated very well by the financial industry and the media over the years. However, there's one criticism I do hear from time to time: "Oh, Dave Chilton, he's that barber guy who just keeps saying the same basic things over and over again — pay yourself first, start now, live within your means."

Exactly.

Pennies From Heaven

INHERITANCES, OR MORE ACCURATELY potential inheritances, are playing a bigger and bigger role in many people's savings decisions. In essence, a lot of Canadians are spending like fools now, hoping to be partially or fully bailed out later by an unusual ally: the Grim Reaper. They are believers in Winston Churchill's pithy observation: "Saving is a fine thing. Especially when your parents have done it for you."

Obviously, I'm not going to advise you to avoid inheritances. In fact, I think it's wise for you to be really, really nice to the elders in your life. For example, I just sent my mother a spectacular bouquet of flowers and, rather cleverly, reminded her on the accompanying card that my sister never does stuff like that.

The problem, of course, is that it's impossible to predict when an inheritance will materialize and how much it will be. People are living to be older and older...and older. What's more, they keep spending their money to the bitter end. The nerve of them!

Will you be 50 when the money flows your way? Sixty? Seventy?

Will there be much left after your parents' retirement-home costs and late-life health care?

What if our deficit-laden government introduces estate taxes? How much of your potential windfall will be confiscated?

Will your benefactors surprise you by leaving most of their estate to a charity? Their pet? Or directly to their grandchildren?

Perhaps poor investment returns will sabotage your loved ones' portfolios, forcing them to dip into a higher percentage of their wealth than anyone anticipated.

As governments throughout the world crank up the printing presses, it's prudent to wonder how much inflation will erode the value of any money coming your way.

That's a lot of uncertainty. What are beneficiaries-in-waiting to do?

Well, what they shouldn't do is count heavily on inheritances when developing their financial plans — at least not without significantly discounting the potential amount. Too much can go wrong. And the most important variable could go right — their parents could live to be 100!

Please look at potential inheritances as future bonuses and not as an excuse to avoid saving today. In fact, don't look at anything as an excuse to avoid saving today.

A Worthwhile Hassle

IN THE CHAPTER "SAVING SAVVY" in *The Wealthy Barber*, Roy Miller advocates keeping a detailed summary of all of your expenses over a period of several months. All of them. No matter how trivial. Whether you use cash, credit cards, automatic withdrawals, whatever — Roy wanted it all captured and later categorized. He argued that the process would provide an eye-opening experience and would alter spending behaviour by shining a light on the hard-earned money that slips between the cracks.

I thought it was an impractical idea. Yes, I wrote it, but I still thought it was an impractical idea. I mean, c'mon, what kind of weirdo is going to carry around a pencil and notepad chronicling every purchase? $1 for a chocolate bar. $16.40 for lunch. $19.95 for a financial book. $60 for gas. As Dave asked in *The Wealthy Barber*, "That's a lot of work, and is there really any benefit? I mean, what can you do about money that's already gone?" I also felt that as long as people were using pay-yourself-first techniques, it really wasn't any of my business how they spent the rest of their money. Truthfully, I only stuck the expense-summary advice in the book because it seemed like something Roy would believe in. I got caught up in my alter ego.

Well, it's embarrassing that once again the fictional me has proven to be wiser than the real me.

I was wrong. Expense summaries do work. In fact, it's amazing how much impact they have. You're probably thinking, "Even so, there's no way I'm going to follow through and track every dime I spend. I might as well skip to the next chapter." Frankly, one of my editors felt the same way, but she's not allowed to skip to the next chapter. Stay open-minded. She changed her mind and you may, too.

The one formerly surefire way to build wealth — pay yourself first — is now often being neutralized by the already-exposed arch-enemy of sound financial planning: excessive spending made possible by easy credit. It's really troubling the number of net-worth statements I see nowadays where an individual or couple has built up a significant RRSP on the Assets side but matched it with an outsized, non-mortgage consumer debt on the Liabilities side. This is something I almost never ran into in the late '80s when I wrote *The Wealthy Barber*. Not coinciden-tally, lines of credit were first pushed aggressively in 1990 and credit-card limits began their ridiculous upward climb at about the same time.

So today, even some pay-yourself-firsters need to cut their spend-ing. Although that's never easy, it's easier if you know where the money is going in the first place. In fact, several behavioural economists point out that the mere act of monitoring expenses tends to reduce spending — even before an austerity plan is put in place. Somehow awareness alone, subconsciously I guess, leads people to be more fiscally responsible. Yes, that sounds a bit "new agey" to me, too, but it's accurate. Literally everyone I've put through this exercise reported that his or her spending soon slowed, despite no conscious effort.

It's quite remarkable.

There's a second reason for my 180-degree turn on spending summaries. They help people not only limit their spending, but also better prioritize it.

We're all dealing with finite resources. It should be our goal to spend our discretionary money on those things and experiences that give us the most joy. We should seek the biggest bang for each hard-earned buck. However, many behavioural economists argue we don't. Instead of comparing how many "joy units" an item will give us relative to an alternative purchase, we rush in: "Hey, this looks neat and the price is fair — I'll take it!"

Obviously, dollar cost is important, but we should also think in terms of opportunity cost. Perhaps the potential purchase's projected four joy units do justify its price, but what if for the same $30, another item would give us seven joy units? Wouldn't that be a wiser choice?

Don't dismiss this as babble (even though I'll concede it sounds like it). It really is a key point. Financial types like me love to focus on wise savers, but there are wise spenders out there, too. They get the most from their money and, no, I don't mean that they're cheap. They view their expenditures as investments and seek the highest available return. A return not measured in dollars or percents, but in joy.

Janet and Greta, the *Looneyspoons* sisters, constantly remind people that it's OK, on occasion, to savour some high-fat, not-so-nutritious food, but make sure it's "splurge-worthy." Don't risk packing on the pounds for anything less than an exceptional piece of your favourite chocolate lava cake. Good spenders bring that same mentality to their buying decisions.

Splurge-worthy. I like that.

Time and time again, I find a spending summary draws attention to all of the money we let slip through our fingers without a "high return." The process leaves participants shaking their heads and vowing to make changes. Much more importantly, they usually honour that vow.

They don't just spend less, they spend better. They become efficient spenders.

Efficient spenders. I like that, too. It's very Roy Miller.

Again, I'll admit that keeping track of every single expense over a multi-month period is a major pain in the butt. I'm lazy — I hate doing things like that. But there are a lot of software programs and apps available today that can dramatically ease the burden. So, yes, I used to think that spending summaries were a waste of energy but, hey, there's no arguing with success. Several people have told me that compiling their summaries has helped them to control (and improve!) their spending more than any other single strategy. A strong testimonial.

Knowledge is indeed power.

Now I'm off to A&W for a Teen Burger. Infinite joy units. Beyond splurge-worthy.

And Furthermore

LISTENING TO THE FEEDBACK of the test readers of the previous chapter was enlightening. About 25 percent of them had already used spending summaries and swore to their effectiveness. Another 25 percent or so were convinced to give the process a try. The final 50 percent politely praised the concept, then quickly changed the subject, apparently unconverted. It's obvious that I need to brush up on my persuasive-writing skills.

Among those who have created summaries, it's interesting that, over and over again, the totals in the same three spending areas seem to have caught them the most off guard: (1) cars; (2) dining out; and (3) little things.

Now, it's important to note that those weren't always the areas where these people spent the most, or even necessarily the areas where they spent the most foolishly. Those were the areas where they spent the most beyond what they thought they were spending.

"Don't people know what their car payments are each month?" you wonder. Well, yes, but when they have two financed cars, they often don't add the payments together to get a genuine feel for their total monthly carrying costs. Strange but true. More relevant, though, is that before this exercise, they had never grouped their car payments with their insurance premiums, maintenance costs and gas charges. When they did, they were absolutely shocked.

We all know that cars are expensive. But few seem to realize just how expensive. Very, very — that's how!

"Let's grab a quick bite" appears to be our new anthem. Yet Canadians consistently underestimate how frequently they sing it. In fact, upon seeing their finished spending summary, several people have protested, "That dining-out figure can't be right — we're not even 'restaurant people.'" But the numbers never lie.

By the way, I'm a self-confessed restaurant person. I can cook only one meal: Shreddies and tea. Understandably, I eat out regularly. In fact, I dine five to seven times a week at The Daily Grill in Waterloo alone. By "alone," I mean as in just that restaurant *and* "alone" as in by myself. Yeah, I know — loser! But, hey, that little plug just got me a free breakfast.

Shock! That's the only way to describe people's reactions to their spending on "little things." Nobody, and I mean nobody, can believe how the purchases of under $20 add up. From magazines to cappuccinos to golf balls to movies to lottery tickets to treats for the kids to greeting cards to batteries to eyeshadow... well, you get the idea. It never ends!

A few years ago, David Bach, a well-known American financial writer, coined the term "latte factor." He argued that by cutting back on a few of those little things, especially those habitual daily purchases, people could save a surprising amount of money. Interestingly, some financial journalists criticized his advice, countering that nobody's ever built up significant wealth a few dollars at a time and, besides, who is David Bach to tell us what temptations we can and can't give in to?

Wow! I was blown away by how out of touch some of these so-called financial experts were. Nobody's ever built up significant wealth a few dollars at a time? Are they kidding? That's exactly how many people do meet their financial goals: a dollar at a time. They pay themselves first, then live within their means by carefully — not obsessively, but carefully — watching their expenses, including the little ones.

Ben Franklin, arguably history's wisest personal-finance expert, summed it up eloquently: "Beware of little expenses. A small leak will sink a great ship."

Furthermore, Bach didn't mean "stop drinking lattes" literally. Really, he was just updating our grandparents' adage: "Look after the nickels and dimes and the dollars will take care of themselves." He wasn't telling people how to spend their money. He was just reminding them that the little expenses collectively aren't so little and to look for some opportunities to scale down where you're not getting a good bang for your buck.

So, we're back to Janet and Greta's "splurge-worthy" again; a basic but important concept regardless of the size of your contemplated expense. "Invest" your spending money where it gives you the best returns. Of course, neither I nor any financial advisor can tell you where that will be. Different strokes for different folks and all that stuff. George Best, the late Manchester United star and renowned partier, perfectly captured our diverse priorities: "I spent a lot of money on booze, birds and fast cars. The rest I just squandered." I laugh every time I read that.

When I first started studying people's spending summaries, I was taken aback by how good savers, just like not-so-good savers, had areas of indulgence and seemingly excessive spending. Frequently, it was travel. Often, it was a hobby like golf. Sometimes, it was my weakness: dining out. Good savers are not passionless robots! They find many things and experiences (usually the latter) splurge-worthy. But they have the common sense and the requisite Grade 2 math skills to recognize that extra spending in one area requires extra discipline in others. That seems to have escaped many in modern society who have instead concluded that extra spending in one area requires extra borrowing in others. Ugh!

Obviously (or maybe not), you can't have it all. It's about choices. It's about trade-offs. And, yes, it's about sacrifices.

Prioritize, think before you spend and don't wear the costume of consumer debt to pretend you're wealthier than you are.

The best way to jump-start this approach, of course? Right! Start keeping a spending summary. Please! (I've run out of ways to convince you and have now resorted to the ultimate rhetorical device — begging.)

By the way, don't let any of this affect how much you spend on books.

The $64,000 Question

HERE IS A QUESTION I DREAD: "How much do I need to set aside each month for retirement?"

Why do I dread it? Well, mostly because the person asking usually hates my response and I like to be liked. But also because the answer depends on a lot of variables and, frankly, on a lot of guesses. There is no one-size-fits-all figure or percentage.

I wish there were, darn it.

Let's start by going back to the basic lesson of Chapter 1: You must create a pool of capital during your working years that can provide a reasonable lifestyle during your retirement years.

Pretty straightforward, right? Not exactly.

At what age will you retire? And at what age will you die? In other words, how long must your pool of capital last?

What will the tax rates be during your retirement years?

How bad will inflation be and what will it do to your purchasing power in your golden years?

How much of your own health-care costs will you be responsible for?

Will government programs such as the Canada Pension Plan (CPP), Quebec Pension Plan (QPP) and Old Age Security (OAS) be altered before you start drawing cheques?

What rate of return can you safely assume you'll earn on your investments over the years?

I have no idea what the answers to those questions are for myself, let alone for you. Nobody else does, either. Yes, financial types can make educated forecasts and, yes, sophisticated software programs and Internet applications can use complex models based on actuarial tables and historical data. But, c'mon, let's be realistic here: We're all guessing. Big-time guessing.

Now, if you promise to die at 82 and to earn 3.9 percent on your investments after taxes and inflation, I'll work around the other questions to give you a reasonably precise needed savings rate. But please don't ruin all of my hard work by breaking your word and living to be 90. Your poverty-stricken final years will make me look bad.

Clearly, the "How much?" question is tricky. Very tricky.

And there's more bad news. The uncertainty is almost certainly going to be replaced by a more negative uncertainty. I'm nearly certain of it.

Why?

Well, people want to retire earlier and earlier. And even if they don't, their employers often want them to.

Life expectancies keep rising and may be about to do so exponentially due to breakthroughs in medical technologies. Just think, you may be married for 80 years!

With our country's challenging fiscal situation and our demographic trends (those pesky baby boomers to support with pensions and health care), there's a good chance that tax rates will rise.

Speaking of government debts, it's hard to believe that with most developed nations in hock up to their grandkids' eyeballs, the printing presses won't be cranked up at some point, and cranked up hard. The number 1 enemy of retirees — inflation — is an inevitable visitor.

For the same reasons, CPP, QPP and OAS may become stingier. If you can survive without them, you just might have to.

Finally, even during good times, most Canadians have under-performed on the investment-return front as we battle both extremely expensive financial products and our own psychological sabotages (much more later). Going forward, we might have to deal with "muddle-through" financial markets fighting the headwinds of excessive public and private debt and the resultant slow economic growth.

No, Broadway will not be making a musical out of this chapter. Did I mention that you may be married for 80 years?

The bottom line is that it's impossible to say how much you should save each month for retirement, but it's probably more than you currently are and maybe even quite a bit more.

Can you see why people hate my response? Heck, I hate my response and I *am* me.

But let's forget me and all of my uncertainty and out-of-character negativity for a minute. What do the other financial writers and experts recommend? What savings rate does the financial industry push? What do actuarial tables say?

Surprisingly, they all offer up a pretty consistent response: somewhere between 10 and 15 percent of your gross income.

Yes, gross income.

Yep, that's quite a bit.

Undeniably, some in the financial industry have a self-interest in pushing you to save more. But the suggested range makes sense for a high percentage of people, alas.

Don't despair, though. It's not as bad as it sounds. Remember: A relatively small cutback in your spending rate can dramatically increase your savings rate. I'm also hopeful that the previous chapters have helped you realize that the cutback needn't affect your happiness.

Actually, I truly believe that you will be happier saving more and spending less. And, no, I'm not drunk as I write this.

Married for 80 years.

Perhaps I will have a drink.

When You Assume

THIS IS A VERY IMPORTANT CHAPTER. Please don't yell, "Finally!"

One of the key assumptions used to determine our required savings rate needs to be examined. You see, most of the formulas used to arrive at the 10 to 15 percent savings level assume we're going to start saving at age 25 and continue unabated until age 65.

Life sometimes interferes.

So, what if you're 35 and haven't yet started building your nest egg?

Or you're 45 and have saved but not at the suggested pace?

Well, there are only two ways to recover: (1) Put aside more than the recommended 10 to 15 percent of your pre-tax income; or (2) Become a brilliant investor, outsmart the investment markets and dramatically outperform the percentage-return assumptions built into the experts' models. That's right — be the next Warren Buffett.

It's probably best not to count on option two.

Yes, that does mean that a late start requires a higher savings rate. How much higher? Often quite a bit.

Hey, don't shoot the messenger! It's the unbeatable power of compounding. Or, more accurately, the lost power of compounding. The opportunity cost of deferred saving never ceases to amaze me and to punish procrastinators.

The following example is very illuminating, but it's also a little depressing. It's similar to those you'll find in other financial-planning books, including *The Wealthy Barber*, but with a kicker that's too often neglected.

Twin brothers open a locksmith business at the age of 25. Things go well right off the bat and Hank, the traditionally responsible brother, begins contributing 8 percent of his $50,000 annual income to an RRSP — $4,000 a year. He sticks with the program for 10 years but then inexplicably buys Maple Leafs' season tickets and can no longer afford to set aside any money. Crazy.

His brother, Simon, parties hard and postpones saving until age 35, coincidentally the age at which Hank stopped. However, Simon sticks with his $4,000-a-year RRSP contribution for an impressive three decades. Both portfolios earn an 8 percent average rate of return compounded annually.

At age 65, Hank's RRSP will be worth $629,741. Simon's will be worth only $489,383.

A Leafs' fan actually comes out on top for once.

Simon saved three times as much money. He saved for 30 years versus Hank's 10. But because Simon started a mere 10 years later — seemingly not that big a deal on a 40-year time frame — he ended up with a much smaller pool of capital.

There's no justice.

Now, let's take the example a step further. This is where it gets really interesting.

Say Hank had stayed sane, watched my awesome Red Wings on TV and kept saving $4,000 a year. Logically, he would finish with $1,119,124. How did I get that? I added his initial total of $629,741 to $489,383 because, as we know from his brother, that's what the additional 30 years of saving would produce.

Hmm. Hank now finishes with 2.29 times as much money as poor Simon. Yikes.

The most powerful way to frame this? Because Simon started to save only a decade later, he now has to save 2.29 times as much per month to catch up to Hank. That's about $9,150 a year — more than 18 percent of his $50,000 income.

Not impossible. But very challenging. Plus, what if Hank had been contributing the recommended 10 to 15 percent instead of 8 percent? Oh my. Simon would be in a world of pain.

I could show the example using a 20-year delay in saving, but I don't want anyone to cry while reading my book.

Admittedly, I left out inflation, and the high rate of return of 8 percent colours the numbers, but you get the point.

Start now! Don't delay! Operators are standing by!

Strangely, a few economists and mathematicians have been pushing the idea of *intentionally* not saving in your early working years because your income is low and your starting-out-in-life costs are high. They advocate ramping up efforts big time in your middle years as your cash flow rises and your costs stabilize.

Do not heed that advice. It may sound great in the classroom but it seldom works in the living room. First, costs have a funny way of never stabilizing. Second, most people aren't going to be able to transition from setting aside nothing to being supersavers at the flip of a switch. Psychologically, that's just not realistic. Finally, I can't get the numbers to work anyway. Am I actually saying that mathematicians are getting their math wrong? Yep. And before you roll your eyes, know that William Bernstein, one of the most intelligent and respected voices in the world of finance, and a former neurologist for good measure, agrees with me. In fact, he's an even harsher critic of the "save late but go big" approach than I am.

Now, my appropriate fear mongering aside, don't panic if you're one of the tardy ones. I've met a lot of Canadians who have recovered from slow starts and done just fine. As Roy Miller advised in *The Wealthy Barber*, "The best time to plant an oak tree was 20 years ago. The second best time is now." Silly barber — the second best time was obviously 19 years ago, but Roy's point is still strong.

The math is clear: Procrastination is your enemy. Save now. Right now. And save a lot.

When I sit down with people who have saved sufficiently throughout their lives, I see three common denominators: (1) They paid themselves first; (2) They started young, or if not, they compensated with increased savings rates; and (3) Their debt management followed the approach outlined in "Owe No!"

That's it.

Nothing fancy. No complicated techniques.

Flossing, exercising and saving.

Common sense and some discipline.

"That Doesn't Apply to Me!"

COUNTLESS TIMES, PEOPLE HAVE explained to me, usually with tremendous passion, why they needn't save as much as the experts recommend.

The funny thing is, in many cases they're right. Betcha didn't think I was going to say that!

To understand why, it's important to look at the bedrock assumption used by most experts to calculate our required savings rate: We'll need between 60 and 70 percent of the average income of our last few working years to have an enjoyable retirement.

Can that range really be appropriate for everyone? We're all so different. Sure, there will be some exceptions. Surprisingly, though, anecdotal evidence from my experiences with retirees and formal research both show those exceptions will be few and far between.

The 60 to 70 percent guideline is pretty darn solid.

Some financial advisors argue that we should shoot for a retirement income *equal* to that of our last few employed years. One hundred percent. Hey, I'm all for aggressive savings targets but that's probably not a necessary or realistic goal for most people.

Remember, in retirement, a number of considerable expenses from our working years probably no longer exist. The kids have moved out. And back in. Then out again for good (we hope). The mortgage and other debts have been paid off. Clothing costs have been reduced and commuting expenses have stopped altogether. And — a frequently forgotten biggie — there's no longer a need to set aside money for retirement. You're there!

Frankly, if you can't live on 60 to 70 percent of your pre-retirement income in that situation, I don't think any book can help you.

Canada Pension Plan, Quebec Pension Plan and Old Age Security will play a role, but the math says most of us should still build a pool of capital capable of spinning off at least 50 to 60 percent of our pre-retirement income.

Ah, but what if you have a defined-benefit (DB) pension plan? Won't its guaranteed retirement payouts lessen your savings needs?

Yes, and probably considerably. Hallelujah!

These pensions derive their name from the fact that their benefits are defined. (What an insightful point!) But defined by what? A formula. The specifics vary from plan to plan but, essentially, you're paid a retirement income based on your years of service, usually the average income of your final few working years and the contributions determined by your sponsor. In most cases, that's your employer, but it could be your union or an insurance company.

Some of these plans are nothing short of financial-planning dreams come true.

For example, I have a friend whose plan will pay her 1.5 percent of her last working-year's salary for each year she has worked for the company. If she ends up spending her entire career there, say 40 years, her pension will pay her 60 percent of her final year's pay as an employee. And she has no deductions from her paycheque!

How great is that? Even without setting aside any additional money from her earnings or having to manage the challenges of investing, she's going to hit the desired 60 percent mark. Sweet! Forget funding an RRSP; she doesn't even have to know how to spell RRSP.

I know what you're thinking: "That lucky, lucky woman doesn't have to read this boring book." How rude.

Many defined-benefit pension plans, though, aren't as generous as the one just described. Perhaps only 40 percent of a lifelong employee's income will be replaced in retirement by the pension's payout. That person will have to do additional saving and learn the ins and outs of the various investment options right along with the rest of us poor, pensionless souls. How much saving? Well, in this case, probably four to five percent of his or her pre-tax income. But every situation is different. If you're a member of a defined-benefit pension plan, thank your good fortune, then sprint down to your human resources department to get all of the details. Working with your financial advisor and some applications on the Internet, you should be able to figure out your required savings rate. Then multiply it by 1.2 to be on the safe side. No, I'm not kidding.

Of course, most of us aren't going to work for the same company throughout our entire career. I shouldn't have to say this, but I know from experience that I do: In those years when you're not a member of a defined-benefit pension plan, you'll have to join the rest of us in Savingsland. On its own, 12 years in even the best defined-benefit plan does not a good retirement make. Sorry.

Speaking of moving from job to job, watch out for "premature evacuation." Your pension contributions and their earnings will vest — that is, you will become their legal owner — after up to five years of full-time employment, depending upon your province. Leaving voluntarily just before vesting takes place might be a very costly move. Know your DB pension's details and recognize that sometimes it pays extremely well to suck it up for a few months.

There is a common misconception about defined-benefit pension plans that needs to be cleared up. Many Canadians think that employees don't make any contributions to their DB plans. That's not always the case. Often participants have significant deductions from their paycheques to help fund their plans. In fact, it could be argued that the employee is even making the employer's contribution. That sounds nonsensical, but when you think about it, all contributions are really part of the compensation plan, a plan that has to be competitive enough to attract the right employees. Instead of taking all of their compensation in current income, the employees are taking some in the form of a defined-benefit pension. Good move. Tax-deductible forced savings.

It seems a lot of us are channelling our "pension envy" into anger at the plans' participants. That's not fair or productive.

This anger is particularly prevalent when government pensions are involved. Yes, these have very generous benefits. And, yes, they're going to cost the country a bundle over the next several decades. And, yes, there is a great divide between the haves and have-nots of government defined-benefit pensions. And, yes, I wish I had one.

But the reality is I don't, so I better save a lot. And the other reality is that we shouldn't be upset with government employees. They negotiated those pension benefits as part of their overall compensation packages. Changing those benefits now would be like retroactively docking them pay for previous years' work.

Blame the government's management and its actuaries, not the employees! These things are incredibly expensive to fund and the investment responsibilities fall entirely on the plans' sponsors. In an extended period of low interest rates or poor stock-market returns, *incredibly* expensive can become *almost impossibly* expensive.

That being said, for the participants, the government defined-benefit plans are fantastic. I love them. Would I tell my kids to choose their career paths just to gain access to one? Of course not. I may tell them to choose their spouses for that reason, though.

I'm kidding. Mostly. Sort of. Not.

Hey, maybe I was too harsh about teachers marrying teachers. Well played, indeed.

"That Doesn't Apply
to Me, Either!"

"HMM," YOU'RE PROBABLY THINKING. "I'm not a member of a defined-benefit pension plan. There must be some other excuse I can dream up for not saving 10 to 15 percent of my pre-tax income. Something? Anything?"

You may be in luck.

There are a few other legitimate reasons for saving at a lesser rate. There are lots of illegitimate reasons, too, but most of us are already intimate with those.

High-income earners, especially ultra-high-income earners, are in a really bizarre position. On the one hand, their big cash flows should make it relatively easy to save to the suggested 10 to 15 percent level. On the other hand, they can get away with saving a lesser percentage because they often don't need 60 to 70 percent of their final working-year's earnings to enjoy an enviable retirement. Two professionals earning a combined $400,000 a year probably don't require a $265,000 annual retirement income to be happy. Some do — you know who you are! — but most don't.

Why? First, because $265,000 is a lot of dough. That's more than $22,000 a month! Second, most big earners dedicate an even larger-than-normal amount of their working-years' incomes to fund expenses that won't exist in retirement. Mortgage payments on a cottage to summer with the kids. Private schools for the kids. Fully funded post-secondary educations for the kids. Riding lessons for the kids. Counselling for the kids who somehow developed a sense of entitlement.

However, I still think top earners should put away at least 10 to 15 percent of their incomes. Save when the saving's good. Life happens. Divorce, bad investment returns, job loss, another divorce...the good times don't always roll on forever. That can be hard to bear in mind while you're living them, but recent, turbulent times prove it's all too true. As Ben Franklin advised: "Save while you may; No morning sun lasts a whole day."

Plus, as I mentioned, it's really not that tough to put aside a good chunk of your earnings when you're pulling in a hefty six-figure income.

Or rather, it shouldn't be. But as my favourite economist, Sherry Cooper of BMO, points out, we have many big earners who aren't saving even five percent. They've confused a high income with wealth and, ironically, that confusion will stop the former from ever becoming the latter.

It's crucial to understand that wealth flows from savings, not from income. And anyone who argues that income and savings are perfectly correlated hasn't studied many people's personal finances. Upper-echelon earners are often more susceptible to the pressures described in the chapters "Consumed With Consumption" and "Status Update." Keeping up appearances frequently overwhelms keeping up savings.

Many experts point out that very low-income earners also needn't save 10 to 15 percent of their wages. It's noted that they'll have a disproportionately large percentage of their working-years' incomes replaced by Canada Pension Plan, Quebec Pension Plan, Old Age Security and, in some cases, the Guaranteed Income Supplement. In fact, sometimes those payments on their own will total more than 70 percent of many low-income-earners' final paycheques. The problem is, that's 70 percent of a very modest number and its associated subsistence lifestyle. What's more, expenses don't tend to fall off as much in retirement for this group as they do for higher earners. They're often renters and that cost will continue in retirement. Also, few are going to be able to spend the money they were formerly saving for retirement because, for good reason, they weren't formerly saving it. Obviously, survival trumps saving. There are no easy answers here, I'm afraid.

A few prominent actuaries have recently argued that some people can save less because their modest retirement-lifestyle plans won't require too significant an income. They point out that many people living on retirement incomes of only 50 percent of their last working-year's pay have adjusted and often seem quite content.

As a pushy pro-saver, it pains me to admit that's true. I can't be a hypocrite here — I'm the one who believes all our spending isn't closely correlated to our happiness. Less consumption doesn't necessarily mean less joy.

However, it's also true that there are a tremendous number of people in that income situation who aren't content. They can't afford to take any trips or spoil their grandkids or fully enjoy some of their favourite hobbies.

They're constantly stressed over their tight financial situations and, with no margin for error, very worried about the return of higher inflation or living "too long."

Exercise caution here. When you're in the saving years, especially the key early ones, there's no way to know definitively what kind of retirement lifestyle you'll want. Best to assume you'll be like most of us and want or need the traditional 60 to 70 percent of your last working-year's income.

Hey, ending up with more than enough isn't the worst problem. Too little, on the other hand, well....

The final exception to the savings rule is also an exception to an earlier caveat. On occasion, some people do know, beyond any reasonable doubt, that they're going to inherit a ton of money before, or in the early part of, their retirements. For example, about a decade ago, after a speech I gave, a relatively young woman approached me with the following scenario: "I know you said we should all be saving, but my grandfather is very ill and doesn't have much longer to live. He's recently sold his business and my share of the estate will be around $15 million. What should I do?"

We've been married for nine years now.

I'm joking, of course. She said no.

Seriously, I told her to go ahead and spend her entire salary...if not more. And you thought I was obsessed with saving and not a fun guy. Wrong. I'm crazy!

It's important to repeat, though, that very few of us are going to inherit huge sums of money. Tremendous uncertainty around inheritances is the norm.

By the way, one of my editors wants to know what kind of geek has a favourite economist.

I'll be misplacing her invoice.

Emergency Fun(ds)

MANY IDEAS IN THE WORLD of personal finance sound great in theory and appear to be logical and well thought through in books, but seldom work in real life.

Exhibit one: emergency funds.

Financial writers love these things. And for good reason. We live in unsettled and unpredictable economic times. Bad things happen. What idiot wouldn't recommend saving at least six to nine months of after-tax income to carry us through rough patches?

This idiot.

Why? Because for 30 years I've watched people, even disciplined people, expand the definition of "emergency" whenever they see something they really, really want and they have the money in the bank to buy it.

Few emergency funds stand a chance against society's innate skill: the ability to rationalize. We can convince ourselves of anything if the result is short-term gratification. It can't be a coincidence that "rationalize" sounds like "rational lies," can it?

All too often, I've seen the situation that follows (and worse!) played out in real life:

EMERGENCY-FUND USE	RATIONALIZED EMERGENCY	TRUTH
Trip to Cancun	"Mike's been so stressed at work, he needs this escape. It will rejuvenate him. He'll come back recharged and ready to go. Yes, it's expensive, but what price health?"	Mike wants to party.
Hot tub	"I really believe this will *save* us money. We'll spend more time at home and we won't ever need a pool. Plus, Mike loves having our friends and neighbours over. I mean, what price happiness?"	Mike wants to party.
Finished basement	"The kids are driving us nuts. Our living room is like a drop-in centre. We need a place to call our own and host friends. Yeah, it is a little more than we budgeted, but what price friendship?"	You guessed it — for a good time, call Mike.

Look, I have no problem with Mike personally. In fact, I wish he lived next door. I do have a problem with his financial plan, though.

Book after book has told Canadians that accumulating several months' worth of income should be our top savings priority. Only when that's accomplished should we move on to RRSPs and other vehicles that can help us reach our long-term goals.

The issue is that the vast majority of people never hit their target of six- to nine-months' income before the funds are diverted to a not-so-emergency emergency. They "go all Mike" on us and have to start the process over again. And again. And again.

Meanwhile, their RRSPs sit in perpetual waiting.

Frankly, my own advice in *The Wealthy Barber* was probably even worse than the conventional wisdom I'm criticizing. I argued that instead of saving to have an emergency fund available, people should just set up a line of credit for the appropriate amount. That way they could direct their savings to more productive areas than low-interest, fully taxable investments and avoid the temptation of a swelling bank account.

Whoops. We've now seen how most of us manage our lines of credit.

It's funny, but even after all these years of studying people's financial plans, I'm still not at all sure how best to deal with emergency funds.

Many experts agree that waiting to build an RRSP until an emergency fund is fully established is foolish. They push us to do both simultaneously. Prudent, definitely. Realistic, doubtful.

One intriguing idea I've seen a few people use successfully is to set up a line of credit where a second signature is required to gain access to the funds. A parent or ultra-responsible friend is recruited and instructed not to co-sign for any borrowing unless the credit holder loses a job or suffers another legitimate setback. Third parties tend to have a stricter definition of "legitimate," thankfully. Of course, this approach is far from perfect. Involving another person always complicates matters. And let's be honest, asking someone to co-sign for a line of credit that you'll borrow against only if you're financially desperate is a bit of a tough sell. In those circumstances, he or she might end up on the hook.

Whatever approach you try, your job security and overall financial situation should play significant roles in determining what emergency-fund amount makes sense. Obviously, two married teachers (married to each other, I mean) with no mortgage probably don't have to worry much. A single, new homeowner working on commission in a highly competitive industry — well, that's a different story.

OK, I'll admit I might not have been a whole lot of help here. But the key point I want to finish with is this: The best way to be prepared for an emergency is to consistently live within your means and keep your debt levels well under control.

Yes, I know it's an ongoing refrain, but aggressive borrowing truly is its own emergency. And it's one, unfortunately, where the alarm often doesn't sound until a second crisis arrives and by then, it's too late.

Money Is Time

WHEN I DISPENSE FINANCIAL lessons from the stage or the page, it's tough to know what's going to stick. Some ideas that I've really liked have fallen on deaf ears — or, more likely, not survived the all-important test of mixing with human nature. Others that I didn't really think would resonate have been put into practice and made a difference.

The adage "A dollar saved is two dollars earned" is a good example. Heck, I thought so little of this maxim that I gave it all of one page in *The Wealthy Barber*.

Mistake. I should have pushed it more aggressively — people who apply this knowledge swear by it.

Remember, when you earn an extra $2 at work, you probably keep only about a buck. There are deductions for taxes, Canada Pension Plan, Employment Insurance, union dues, benefits and so on. It all adds up.

Judicious shoppers often "re-frame" the cost of an item by figuring out how long they would have to work to earn the money, post-deductions, to buy it. Not only does executing that thought process buy them a minute or two for their "lizards" to calm down, but it also makes them more aware of an important concept: When we buy something, we're really spending time, not money.

Say what?

Well, initially we traded our time to get the money and now we're trading that money to get the whatever. So, actually we're paying time for the whatever.

Know what you make per hour after deductions, do a quick calculation and ask yourself before a purchase, "Do I really want to work x hours to pay for this?" Thinking this way will truly help you exercise more restraint and be more discerning.

It will make you a wiser spender.

As Cicero noted, "Most men do not understand how great a revenue is economy."

Some Experience Required

EARLIER, I TALKED ABOUT HOW neither I nor any financial advisor can tell you where best to spend your money. You have to follow your passions and "invest your spending money where it gives you the best returns." That, of course, will vary widely from person to person.

Now I'm going to completely contradict myself and tell you where to spend and not spend your money — only in a general sense, though.

Spend more on experiences and less on stuff.

That's it. Follow that one simple guideline and you will be happier. Both anecdotal evidence and formal studies verify that you'll get more emotional bang for your buck.

Elizabeth Dunn, a social psychologist and assistant professor at the University of British Columbia, explained to the *Boston Globe*: "Just because money doesn't buy happiness doesn't mean money cannot buy happiness. People just might be using it wrong."

She and other psychologists and anthropologists are advancing an interesting theory on society's traditionally weak wealth-for-happiness exchange rate: Our wiring, dating back to prehistoric times, leads us to value stuff over experience and ourselves over others. Our ancestors' struggles with scarcity and its first cousin, survival, have programmed us to instinctively emphasize things over all else. The spending that seems to make us happiest, though, follows a completely different path. It's a trade of money for rewards less tangible but much more valuable: excitement, memories, good feelings and camaraderie.

Most things we buy in modern times not only don't help us survive, but don't even help us thrive. Why? Well, one of the big reasons is our old friend, declining marginal utility. When sensory cells are exposed to the same stimulus repeatedly, they get bored and stop firing.

Our new fridges, watches and cars go from "wow" to "whatever" remarkably quickly.

Our rather odd conventional response? "Hmm, more things didn't make me happier — I should buy even more things."

Ah, the materialism treadmill.

On the other hand, many experiences truly bring lasting joy to our lives. Leaf Van Boven, an associate psychology professor at the University of Colorado at Boulder, summarized his studies: "We generally found very consistent evidence that experiences made people happier than material possessions they had invested in."

That makes sense for many reasons. First, experiences don't grow mundane; they don't create habituation. In fact, it's quite the opposite — they offer us a break from the same old, same old. They rescue us from routine and, therefore, excite us.

They also tend to be social by nature and we're at our happiest sharing good times with friends and loved ones. Heck, we're often extremely happy even reliving (and embellishing, of course) the experiences over and over again. We love stories, and experiences create them — and not just any stories, but unique ones where we're the stars.

Van Boven also noted that our experiences don't lead to the inevitable can't-win comparisons that our stuff does. Our new large-screen TV may lose its lustre when our brother-in-law trumps us with his eight-seat home theatre. But the great times and cherished memories of our family trip to Florida aren't at all diminished by our neighbours' vacation to Paris.

I think another important part of the "experience experience" (pardon the expression) is the incredible joy of anticipation. It's motivating and uplifting to know that a great dinner out is only a week away. Or that you'll be taking your son to his first NHL game next month. Or that soon you'll be meeting your best friend in P.E.I. for a golf trip. I love that stuff — or should I say that non-stuff. Heck, being excited during the time leading up to an event is one of the best parts of the whole experience. Anticipating a fun time *is* a fun time!

Let's be clear here: I'm not advising you to become a spendthrift and blow all your money on experiences. You still have to save. But with the money you can truly afford to spend, you may want to adjust your stuff/experience ratio.

I could drive this point home with thoughts from some of the best minds in history, because everyone from Plato to Churchill to Franklin to Buffett has offered wisdom on remembering what's genuinely important and letting that guide your spending. However, my favourite quote on the matter comes from a bumper sticker I saw in Saskatoon: "The best things in life aren't things."

A Final Reminder

I RECOGNIZE IT'S EXTREMELY BAD form to quote a book within the very same book but, hey, when you say as few insightful things as I do, it's important to repeat them:

> One of the most damaging misconceptions in personal finance is that saving for the future requires sacrifices today that lessen people's enjoyment of life. Surprisingly, it's quite the opposite! People who live within their means tend to be happier and less stressed. That's true not only for the obvious reason — they know their financial futures look bright — but also because they're not consumed with consumption. They're not in the emotionally and financially draining race to acquire the most stuff they possibly can. A race that, it should be noted, has no finish line and thus no winner.

Although I've made my share of money mistakes, as you'll see in the next section, trying to buy happiness isn't one of them. I live a very modest life. My house is 1,300 square feet, including the basement, and there's no garage. I don't need one — nothing to store. A few years ago, a couple of teenagers broke into my place while I was on a speaking tour. Boy, they must have been disappointed. I have visions of one turning to the other and pleading, "Hey, go back to our car and grab this guy a stereo or something — he's obviously struggling!"

Yet my friends will tell you that despite my humble lifestyle, I'm one of the happiest guys going. Interestingly, I would argue that my positive disposition doesn't exist "despite" my humble lifestyle, but instead partially *because* of it.

I'm never stressed about keeping up. I truly couldn't care less what others have. I don't need the latest and the greatest. My wardrobe proves that I'm not image-conscious. When not working, I'm focused on the more important things in life like my hockey pool, my daughter's choice of boyfriends, crushing my son in tennis or cheering on my beloved Detroit Tigers at my mom and dad's place.

Speaking of my mom and dad, they totally get it. In fact, they're even happier than I am — it's annoying. They don't have a flat-screen TV, granite countertops, a walk-in closet, an iPad, a fancy car or hardwood floors. Yet miraculously, they're upbeat, well-adjusted people. How can that possibly be? Don't they realize that today's society is all about materialism?

What *do* they have? Well, an active social life. A loving family. The world's greatest dog. Cryptic crosswords. An addiction to bridge. A strong desire to help. An endless supply of Cadbury Mini Eggs. Reasonable health. Loads of perspective. And each other (a much bigger asset for my dad than for my mom, I might add). They also have the one thing that many of my "wealthy" friends will never possess: They have enough.

Jean-Jacques Rousseau (the Swiss-born French philosopher) understood the psychology behind my mom and dad's contentment, long before their births. In 1754, he argued that wealth is not an absolute; instead, it is relative to desires. When we covet things we can't afford, we grow poorer regardless of our incomes. Conversely, when we're satisfied with what we have, we are truly wealthy.

By the way, my mom and dad aren't cheap. They're not even what I would call thrifty. They go out for dinners, spoil their grandkids, take trips and, on occasion, buy even a luxury item. But they live within their means. They control their desires not through rigid self-discipline — that's tough to sustain — but through an awareness of what should be obvious to us all: Happiness flows from relationships, health and making a difference, not from a $1,000 solid-brass kitchen faucet.

American theologian Hosea Ballou once noted: "Real happiness is cheap enough, yet how dearly we pay for its counterfeit." Don't make that mistake. Be like my mom and dad and *live well* within your means — you'll be richer in every sense of the word!

Random Thoughts
on Personal Finance

Common Themes

I HAVE TO ADMIT THAT THIS PART of the book is a little different. In fact, I'm not even sure exactly how to describe it.

It's kind of all over the map. Actually, not "kind of" — it *is* all over the map. Some big-picture stuff, some minutiae. Some conventional wisdom, some offbeat perspectives. Some numbers, some psychology. Some fluff, some depth. Some dos, some don'ts.

I guess it's really a collection of a few of my opinions and observations on the world of personal finance. Certainly not all of them will apply to any one reader, but I'm hopeful that you'll find the vast majority interesting and that together they'll help you think more wisely about your money.

Despite the word "random" in this section's title, there are a couple of common themes running through many of the pieces that follow.

The first is that sound financial planning is surprisingly straightforward — nothing more than a combination of common sense, vanilla products and time-tested principles. Honest!

You don't have to spend hours researching on the Internet every night. (I do, but that's for my hockey pool.)

You don't have to possess great math skills. Heck, last week I asked one of the most successful investors I know what 7^3 is.

He's still working on it. On the other hand, Isaac Newton was notoriously bad with his money.

You don't have to master the strange jargon of the financial world. Yes, it's important to know some basic terms but beyond those, there's no correlation between an individual's vocabulary and his or her money-management abilities. Years ago, I congratulated a fellow on his astute retirement plan. His response? "Yeah, my RSVP is rockin'!" Hey, party on, bro.

I will admit that there are a lot of complex products in the financial arena. Many involve hours of reading and sometimes even advanced calculus to fully understand. Others are based on arcane associations of assumptions, algorithms and acronyms.

They don't work. Avoid them.

Leonardo da Vinci once stated, "Simplicity is the ultimate sophistication." Smart guy — I'm surprised he didn't accomplish more.

The second recurring theme is that human nature matters. Big time. It influences us in a variety of ways as we manage our money — few of them positive. For example, to work its wonders, a financial plan requires us to be disciplined and patient. That's a big problem because most of us, well, aren't. We're easily both distracted and scared.

We need to account for our emotional weaknesses, and to whatever extent possible, protect against them. Yet frequently, financial advice assumes we'll always behave in a completely rational manner. We won't.

Keep it simple and get out of your own way.

Common themes that need to become common practice.

An Easy Choice

Prospective Advisor #1: "Our models dictate that you should be overweight in equities right now. We'd emphasize emerging markets to capitalize on their growing middle classes, U.S. home builders to play the coming rebound in housing starts and Canadian resource stocks to partake in the commodity boom. Our economist is confident that the central bank won't tighten imminently and that the European debt crisis is manageable. Although we're worried about the upcoming German elections and next week's CPI data, retail sales are reflecting more consumer confidence and that should provide a tailwind."

Prospective Advisor #2: "I have no idea where markets or the economy are headed in the short term. Nor does anyone else here. Our chief economist is brilliant, articulate and wrong more often than right. Great golfer, though."

Run, don't walk, to advisor #2.

There are a lot of very sharp people in the financial industry. The problem is that a dangerous number of them think being intelligent is synonymous with being clairvoyant. It isn't.

No one knows where markets will be in six months, what China's inflation rate is about to do or which currencies are soon to "break out on the upside."

Stop listening to people who think they do.

If your financial plan's success is contingent on accurately predicting the future, you're in trouble. Uncertainty rules. That's precisely why it's wise to build a balanced, diversified portfolio and focus on the long term.

Advisor #1 may be smart, but advisor #2 is smarter. Much.

A Cool Rule

I WAS FIRST EXPOSED TO "THE RULE OF 72" in my second year of university. This will make me sound very geeky (again), but it was love at first sight.

The rule simply states:

$$\text{The years to double your money} = \frac{72}{\text{rate of return compounded annually}}$$

So, if you grow your money at 8 percent compounded annually, it will take you 9 years to double your money (72/8).

At 12 percent it would take you only 6 years (72/12).

At 6 percent it would take you 12 years (72/6).

At 72 percent it would take you 1 year. Whoops — that's not right. Obviously, you'd need a 100 percent return to double your money in 1 year.

Hmm. Maybe "The Rule of 72" would be more appropriately called "The Guideline of 72 That Doesn't Work Well For Extreme Rates of Return."

Regardless, the rule does provide a good approximation of doubling time for rates from 2 to 18 percent. Apply it to higher returns and it starts getting a bit wacky. But, hey, if you're consistently compounding your money at more than 18 percent a year, I should be reading your book, not the other way around.

On the low side, I'm not sure if it works for 1 percent or not. I have a broken calculator and I don't feel like figuring out on paper what 1.01^{71} is, especially with *Modern Family* starting in 10 minutes. The general rule, though, is that if you're growing your money at only 1 percent a year, it will double-over about 20 years after you do.

There are a couple of good lessons that flow from playing around with this rather cool rule.

My parents have owned their home for almost 48 years. They bought it for $19,800 and it's now worth about $320,000. Seems pretty impressive. But what's "The Rule of 72" say? Well, the house value doubled from 20 grand to 40, then 40 to 80, then 80 to 160 and, finally, from 160 to 320. That's 4 doubles in 48 years or 1 every 12 years. That's a compounded rate of return of 6 percent a year.

My mom and dad were surprised that their return *only* averaged 6 percent. It seemed like a lot more growth. But 48 years is a long time for compounding to work its magic.

Some folks aren't just surprised when I perform this type of calculation for them, they're also borderline annoyed. They insist their investment returns must be higher than our mathematical shortcut indicates. Who are these bold deniers who have the audacity to challenge my beloved "Rule of 72"?

Cottage owners, usually.

For example, a few years ago, an elderly couple explained to me that their cottage, purchased for $50,000, was now worth $200,000. "An incredible investment that can't be matched by anything else. Don't you agree?" the husband challenged me.

"Well, it depends on how long you've owned it," I cautioned.

"Forty glorious years!" the wife responded.

"That works out to about 3.6 percent a year," I calculated using my trusty rule. (They averaged a double every 20 years and 72/20 equals 3.6.) "Plus," I added, "you have to account for all your ongoing expenses, such as property taxes, utilities and maintenance. And did you ever spend money renovating?"

From the looks on their faces, you'd think I had just poked them with a sharp stick. This reinforced something that, through many similar experiences, I should have long since internalized: Never ever try to rationally discuss the math of cottage ownership with cottage owners. Never. Ever.

The bigger lesson, though, evidenced by applying "The Rule of 72," is that seemingly small differences in rates of return can make a huge difference in the wealth created over time.

Hard-to-believe huge.

Impossible-to-overstate-the-importance-of huge.

Let's say you were starting out with $10,000 in your registered retirement savings plan (RRSP). You invest the money without learning the basics or developing a plan. Over the years, you pay little attention to costs and on several occasions let your emotions get the best of you. In short, you act like most of us. You go on to average a 4 percent rate of return compounded annually.

Your best friend, who invests $10,000 at the same time, manages to mix together common sense and discipline and averages an 8 percent return compounded annually.

"Whatever," you think. "So he ends up with a little more money. Good for him, he's a great guy. No biggie."

Actually, you'd be right if you were talking about a one-year time period. You'd end up with $10,400; he'd have $10,800. What's $400 between friends? He would probably take you and your spouse out for dinner.

Ah, but what if the money was left alone for 18 years? You'd have $20,000 because at 4 percent, money doubles every 18 years.

He'd have $40,000! Yep, at 8 percent, money doubles every 9 years — 2 doubles and, presto, 10 is 40.

How can that be? You both worked equally hard and made the same sacrifices to save the original $10,000. You practiced the impressive restraint that he did and avoided the temptation to raid your RRSP. Sure, you could have invested more wisely, but it's not like buddy boy was posting spectacular double-digit returns.

It's not fair.

And it gets worse.

Thirty-six years in, nearing retirement, things have turned downright ugly. Your original $10,000 is now $40,000 (10 x 2 x 2). His is now $160,000 (10 x 2 x 2 x 2 x 2).

You're dog-sitting for him while he and his wife travel through the vineyards of Northern Italy for the second time in six months. "We just had to see them in the fall," he explains.

Your bitterness reinforces economist Charles Kindleberger's opinion: "There is nothing so disturbing to one's well-being and judgment as to see a friend get rich."

I play around with this kind of comparison frequently, yet it still blows me away that the former best friend forever (FBFF) ends up with so much more money. Even more troubling, I see similar situations in real life all the time.

Albert Einstein once declared, "The most powerful force in the universe is compound interest." Harnessing that power efficiently is what good investing is all about.

Modestly better returns make for dramatically better retirements. And "The Rule of 72" proves it.

The Illusion of Wealth

TEN YEARS AGO OR SO, WHILE flying from Toronto to Vancouver, I had the pleasure of sitting beside an erudite, older gentleman. He was heading out West to meet his recently born granddaughter and I was on my way to give a speech on Vancouver Island.

When he asked me what I did for a living, I explained that I tried to use stories and humour to take the intimidation out of financial planning.

"Like that *Wealthy Barber* fellow?" he asked.

"Exactly like him," I laughed.

He smiled and admitted that he had never read my book but said that his kids swore by it. (OK, he may have said they swore *at* it.)

Anyway, we struck up a four-hour conversation on all things money. Yeah, I know, pray you never sit beside me on an airplane. But it was his idea, really.

He had his investment-account summaries and a fairly up-to-date set of net-worth and cash-flow statements in his briefcase. This guy takes his finances seriously. Pathetically, I was excited to take a look.

It was all very impressive. He may not have read *The Wealthy Barber*, but he could have written it. He and his wife paid themselves first, built significant RRSPs and were debt-free.

One thing confused me, though. He had their home's value listed at only $100,000. Hey, I love small houses but, c'mon, these were Torontonians. What did they live in — a garage? Then I noticed that their property taxes and utility bills were far from low. What was I missing?

"Well, our house is currently worth about $600,000," my new friend began. "But we're planning on moving to a condominium in a couple of years. It'll cost us around $400,000. That will be our last stop, by the way. Because the expenses there will be higher with the monthly fees, I've allotted $100,000 of the $200,000 excess to spin off an income to cover the increased costs. So, essentially, we have only $100,000 in our house that we'll be able to convert to a true investment asset. Is that a strange way to look at it or does it make sense to you?"

Perfect sense.

In fact, I wish everyone would follow his logic. As the values of their homes have grown, many Canadians have fooled themselves into thinking they're in much better financial shape than is truly the case.

We have a lot of people heading toward retirement "house rich, investment poor." So, you wonder, won't they just sell and move to much smaller dwellings?

Maybe. But it's a myth that everyone wants to downsize later in life. Obviously some do, but many others hate moving and enjoy established relationships in their neighbourhoods. Their homes and communities are a big part of their identities.

My mom and dad, for example, have no plans to leave their home until they die (at that point, we'll insist). They'll opt for assisted care over moving. The fact that their home's value has risen by hundreds of thousands of dollars while they've lived there, strangely, is of no financial consequence to them.

Well, actually, it is. As real-estate prices in Kitchener-Waterloo have climbed, they've dragged my parents' property taxes and insurance premiums up with them. Mom and Dad should be cheering for a market pullback!

My sister and I will be the real beneficiaries of their increased home value. To that end, we're constantly urging them to stop socializing so much and upgrade their kitchen.

Even when people do move to a less expensive home, it's often not the windfall they might expect. Look at my seatmate's story. Few of us are willing to take a huge step back in lifestyle at any point, even in retirement, and our houses play a major role in defining those lifestyles. I know a lot of people whose move down, um, hasn't been. Plus, don't forget sales-agents' commissions, lawyers' fees, land-transfer taxes, moving costs, and so on and so on. Together, they take a big bite out of the gross freed-up capital.

Ironically, the people who are fiercely passionate about owning the biggest, most expensive home they can "afford" are often the ones forced to trade way down later in life. Ouch. They come face to face with a very basic truth: You can live in your house or you can invest the proceeds from its sale, but you can't do both simultaneously.

As I mentioned earlier, I'm all for home ownership in most cases. But on its own, a house — even a spectacular, fully paid-for house — does not a retirement plan make.

A Controversial Solution

SO, AN ALARMING NUMBER OF retired Canadians have fully paid-for homes but insufficient savings. Though they're struggling to pay the bills, they don't want to downsize.

It's a tough situation but perhaps they *can* have their cake and eat it too.

How? By taking out a reverse mortgage.

"What's that?" you ask. Like a conventional mortgage, it's a loan made to a home or condo owner where his or her property serves as collateral. But with a reverse mortgage, the borrower does not have to make ongoing payments on the loan and the balance isn't due until the home is sold.

Really, it's a way to tap into one's home equity without moving.

The problem is that it's an expensive way. First, the senior homeowner has to pay for an appraisal and independent legal advice — pretty standard stuff. But then there are also closing costs of well over $1,000 payable to the lender. That's annoying.

The big issue, though, is how quickly the debt grows. Interest rates on reverse mortgages are significantly higher than those on conventional mortgages. Plus, and this is key, the borrower is turning finance's most powerful force — compounding — into an enemy instead of a friend.

Remember "The Rule of 72"? At 5 percent, the amount owed will double in about 14 years. At 10 percent, and, yes, we could see those rates again, the balance will almost quadruple in the same time.

Yikes. No wonder many financial professionals are uncomfortable with this product. They've been trained their entire careers to harness compounding's magic, not to fight it. They note that if interest rates rise significantly or the real-estate market softens, a borrower's equity could be completely wiped out. "You'll be spending your kids' inheritance," is a common refrain.

True, yet I still think reverse mortgages are, on occasion, a viable solution to the "house-rich, investment-poor" problem.

Frankly, many seniors need to focus on their own challenging financial situations and worry less about their beneficiaries' futures. Sure it would be great to leave money to your family, but not if it means living out your final years hand to mouth or being miserable over having to move.

That said, when my father asked me whether he and my mom should look at reverse mortgages, I replied, "They're illegal in Canada, Dad." Joking, I wouldn't do that. My sister would, though. No, she wouldn't either — I just stuck that in to make her look bad.

I had an interesting phone call from a thoughtful advisor last year. He conceded that he is normally very hesitant to recommend reverse mortgages, but felt he may have come across an exceptional case. An elderly client had been diagnosed with cancer and given only a few years to live. She was adamant about not moving but couldn't afford proper in-home care on her low income. She also wanted to help her grandson out with his university costs. Initially, the advisor thought it was a rare, ideal time for a reverse mortgage, which would allow her to stay in the house and free up the needed funds. However, after thinking it through, he instead suggested a home-equity line of credit (HELOC). He pushed her to borrow only as needed and to service the debt through writing cheques on the line of credit itself. Sounds a little crazy at first blush, but it makes sense. Both her legal fees and her interest rate would be lower than with a reverse mortgage.

I'll admit reverse mortgages have several drawbacks and shouldn't be used without looking at all the other alternatives carefully. And even when they seem appropriate, a HELOC may be a better move. But don't rule them out — they are one possible solution to an all-too-common problem.

Oh, one more thing: Based on the reverse-mortgage TV commercials airing in both Canada and the States, it appears that only extremely good-looking seniors are eligible. And they must own either a golden retriever or a rose garden.

Dashed Hopes

A BUDDY OF MINE, DAVE KNAPP, once asked me where race horses fit into a financial plan.

They don't.

Many years ago, I talked a number of skeptical friends into purchasing a standardbred horse. That's the breed that races in harnesses at a trot or pace.

The 18 of us parted with $2,500 each. We spent most of the $45,000 on a gorgeous American horse, Dash Lauxmont, and planned to cover ongoing expenses with the rest.

Dash broke his leg the day we bought him. Seriously.

We knew these are fragile animals. We were all fully aware of the high risk of injury. But, c'mon, the first day? You've got to be kidding.

The trainer delivered the bad news over the phone from New Jersey: "Dave, I don't know how to tell you this, but Dash was stomping his foot in the trailer and snapped his cannon bone. It's not good...not good at all."

"Well, Brad," I calmly began, "obviously, it's horrible for the horse but we're covered financially. As you advised, I insured Dash this morning as soon as we hung up the phone."

"That's not going to help. The policy won't pay unless Dash is dead."

"Shoot him," I logically suggested. "Isn't that what's done?"

"Oh, no," Brad replied. "We don't do that anymore unless the horse is in permanent pain and it would be inhumane to let him suffer. No, we'll nurse Dash back to health, but he'll probably never race again."

"Shoot me," I then begged.

I was devastated and embarrassed. And for good reason. I had picked up the investors' cheques just the day before. How could I, a mere 24 hours later, tell them that I'd already lost most of their money? No nights at the races. No daily doubles. No Little Brown Jug. Nothing.

"Don't give up quite yet," Brad consoled me. "We'll send Dash to the Kawartha Downs area. I know some trainers there who will work him out in a huge pool. Swimming — that could do the trick. It's the same motion as running but it doesn't put any stress on the fracture. Yeah, it's a long shot, but who knows?"

Even visions of Dash in a Speedo were less off-putting than the thought of calling my buddies. I gave my approval.

Well, months went by without even an update. Had Dash drowned? Did they let him in the pool within 20 minutes of eating? I couldn't take not knowing, so I called the facility's manager.

"Oh, he's a marvellous swimmer," the upbeat lady comforted me. "Beautiful to watch. Delightful. Makes friends easily...."

Basically, Dash was at summer camp having a fabulous time. Unfortunately for us, it was expensive and he didn't come from a wealthy family.

Then, a miracle.

Brad called with the incredible news: "Dash is healed — he'll be racing in six weeks!"

Was I pumped! All 18 of us were. When the big night arrived, we were out in full force. Some guys rented limos. Some wore tuxes. Some smoked fancy cigars. The evening was pure magic.

Until Dash arrived.

The handlers had trouble settling him into the starting gate. But not nearly as much trouble as our driver had getting him out of it.

Perhaps Dash didn't hear the gun. Water in his ears, I suspect. As the other horses neared the first turn, our boy was apparently still visualizing. I wondered if any horse had ever been lapped. Eventually, he sauntered from the gate and leisurely headed out. When your horse stops and waves, it's not a good sign.

Things didn't get better with time. Last, last, last, last. Race after race, Dash provided almost surreal consistency. When he finally broke through and finished second last, we were accused of doping. He didn't pace so much as he shuffled. His movement eerily resembled the moonwalk. The only good news was that at this speed there was no risk of reinjury.

Had it not been pre-smartphone days, I'm sure our driver would have been texting during the races. One night Dash was so slow he actually got in the winner's circle photo. Great keepsake.

Much like the movie *Free Willy*, we dreamt of returning Dash to his natural habitat — the water. But tragically, we had run out of money.

What to do? We convened a meeting where I suggested giving Dash to a local farmer. One of the partners objected, "I don't want to give him away; I want to race him."

"Go ahead, you'll probably beat him," another snickered.

Eventually, Dash ended up in Detroit. Perhaps he worked the birthday-party circuit. Believe me, no children would have been in danger.

Showman Billy Rose once advised, "Never invest your money in anything that eats...."

Words to live by.

A Misunderstood Shortcut

WOW, I COULDN'T BELIEVE HOW annoyed some readers were because I didn't include an index in *The Wealthy Barber*. Especially librarians. One from California wrote, "No index? You, sir, should be shot!" And that was from a left-leaning state; I shudder to think what the Texans wanted to do to me.

So it's a bit ironic that I'm now going to discuss what an index is. But, of course, the kind of index I'm talking about here has nothing to do with the pages at the back of a book. No, what we're looking at in this chapter is the type of index used in the statistical world: A single number that summarizes a collection of data and often serves as a benchmark for comparison.

Sounds complicated. Isn't.

Yet very few people truly grasp this concept. In fact, I recently asked a group of financial types what an index is and got more than a few crazy answers, including "a finger."

Think of an index as an aid. A shortcut. A time saver.

All totals are indices (or indexes). So are all averages. And all medians.

A golf handicap is an index. The inflation rate is an index. Mrs. Landers' class average is an index. Your career-earnings total is an index.

Anybody can make up an index. I could take my 20 closest friends, total the number of books they read in a year, figure out the average and call that figure the CFBI (Chilton Friend Book Index). It would not be an impressive figure, I assure you.

Hey, you could calculate the equivalent index for your friends and we could compare. Or I could track the CFBI year after year and see if my friends are becoming better read. How likely would that be? Never mind.

The financial world creates and uses indices all the time. Thank goodness. Without them, it would be impossible to effectively communicate and compare the industry's overwhelming volume of data.

For example, one of the most common questions — "How did the stock market do today?" — would be virtually impossible to answer. There are thousands of publicly traded companies, and reciting all of their closing prices would be quite a chore.

Ah, but with an index, the response is as simple as, "The S&P/TSX Composite was up 1.1 percent."

Easy-peasy, as my not-so-eloquent daughter would say.

The S&P/TSX Composite is the Canadian equity markets' best-known index. It's one figure, a weighted average, that summarizes lots of data — the share prices of about 250 of Canada's largest public companies.

There are a number of ways companies can be weighted in an index. They can all be given equal weightings and, on occasion, you'll see that. It seems odd, though, that a two percent move in the price of a relatively small company would have the same effect on an index's value as a two percent move in the price of the biggest. But whoever designs the index sets the rules.

Most equity indices are "cap-weighted." Nothing tricky here. Cap is short for market capitalization, which is calculated by simply multiplying the number of shares a company has outstanding by its market price per share. If company X is worth three times as much as company Y, X receives three times the weighting in determining the index.

Makes good sense.

The S&P/TSX Composite is cap-weighted, as are most of the world's major indices.

An index could also weight each company based on its share price. A firm trading at $30 would carry three times the impact of one trading at $10. But what if the $10-a-share company had nine million shares outstanding and the $30-a-share company had only one million? Hmm. The smaller company would have triple the weighting of the bigger company, despite having only one-third of its market capitalization.

Clearly, weighting by share price is a goofy idea. Curiously, though, that's how one of the world's most famous indices, the Dow Jones Industrial Average, is structured.

Weird.

There are indices for bonds, commodities and real estate, too. Plus, there's an index for a seemingly endless number of sub-sets of each of the asset classes. From emerging-market stocks to big-dividend payers to corporate bonds to agricultural com-modities — there's an index (or several) out there.

But it's key to note again that all of them have two things in common: (1) They are single numbers that summarize a collec-tion of data; (2) Somebody, or somebodies, made them up. He/she/they chose the contributing components, decided on the weighting approach and set the rules.

Frequently, I'll hear, "I want to buy such and such an index." Not possible. Remember, it's just a number — an abstract con-cept. What you can do is buy the components of an index in their prescribed weightings. Doing this on your own is a major hassle, but there are mutual funds (not shockingly called "index funds") and exchange-traded funds (ETFs) that will do it for you inexpensively.

The financial industry often terms index-fund investors "passive" and all others "active." I've never been comfortable with those labels. There are many Canadians who buy and hold several companies' shares indefinitely. These investors almost never trade — they are truly passive, yet they're branded active. And nowadays we have many other Canadians who jump in and out of index funds and ETFs trying to time the markets or play the hot sector. They're not passive — they're *hyper*active. They're not just sitting back, they're making things happen. Things like commissions, higher taxes and below-average returns, for example.

You've probably noticed that this chapter has been a little different. There haven't been any deep insights or unique perspectives. (OK, so it hasn't been *that* different.) But understanding what an index is makes following the financial markets more interesting and more fun.

Plus, now you can sound in the know at a party by opining: "I think it's ridiculous that the Dow is a price-weighted index; cap-weighting makes so much more sense."

Then again your conversation partner may respond, "Good point. I've been looking at the MSCI EAFE but I'm also drawn to fundamental indices and inverse ETFs."

On second thought, it's probably best to keep this to yourself.

Incredibly Interesting Math

"AH," YOU'RE THINKING, "an oxymoron for a chapter title."

Nope — I guarantee you're going to find the numbers and logic that follow very interesting. The math is straightforward but the lesson is profound. And it's one that receives far too little attention.

When you invest in the stock market, you have two choices: (1) You can buy an index fund or exchange-traded fund (ETF) that matches the market's returns (boring); or (2) You can try to beat the market's returns (exciting).

The vast majority of us go with the latter. We weren't raised to settle for average. We all want to be above average. All of us. Above average.

But that's a problem. A mathematical impossibility. On average we have to be, well, average.

In other words, the aggregate return of investors trying to beat the market *must* match the market's return.

Please trust me here — no matter how boring that statement seems (and it seems pretty darn boring), it's absolutely key that you grasp it. In fact, it's so important that I'm going to repeat it: The aggregate return of investors trying to beat the market *must* match the market's return.

It's a mathematical certainty. It can be no other way.

We can't all be above-average investors. The effort to outperform the market is a zero-sum game. There will be winners and there will be losers and they'll cancel each other out. That will be the case even if all the investors are extremely intelligent.

I'm brutal with analogies, but this one may help drive the point home. If Major League Baseball's 30 teams are each managed by one of the greatest leaders in the history of the game, collectively they will end up with the same record as they would if they are led by 30 little kids who don't know where second base is. Either way, every game is still going to produce a winner and a loser. The league will play .500 ball regardless.

Let's look at an oversimplified example of how this ignored truth plays out and why it matters.

Assume there are four mutual funds and each controls one-quarter of the money invested in an imaginary stock market. The first is an index fund that owns every stock on the exchange proportionate to its market value. In other words, it's matching the market. The second fund is managed by the world's most famous investor, Warren Buffett. The third is managed by Buffett's real-life business partner and one of my heroes, Charlie Munger. The fourth and final fund is managed by the brilliant hedge-fund operator, George Soros.

So, 25 percent of the invested capital is happy to match the market and 75 percent, all under outstanding stewardship, is attempting to beat the market.

My mom has $30,000 available and decides to invest it in equities. Here are a few of her options:

(1) She could buy stocks on her own.
(2) She could put the entire $30,000 in the index fund.
(3) She could place $10,000 with each of the legendary managers.

(4) She could put the entire $30,000 with one manager.

If Mom opts to go it on her own, she's crazy. Remember, together she, Buffett, Munger and Soros must earn the same return as the market — the return she can achieve through the index fund. If she hopes to exceed that return, she'll have to outperform the combined efforts of the three investment geniuses. Frankly, that's a far-fetched notion.

If she goes for Door #2, buys the index fund and matches the market, she's *guaranteed* to tie the aggregate performance of the three gurus, as we've learned that performance *must* also match the market's return. If Buffett outperforms by 4% and Soros outperforms by 1%, Munger *must* underperform by 5%.

How cool is that? My mom can kick back, buy a market-matching index fund and keep up with a team of three of the greatest investment minds of all time. This despite the fact that she thinks of stocks only as broths used in soups.

Basic math but still hard to believe, isn't it?

If Mom elects to split her money up evenly among the three managers — the third option — we all now know what *must* happen: She'll match the market and end up in the same position as she would if she had just bought the index fund.

The final alternative, putting the entire $30,000 with one manager, might or might not work out well. One or maybe two of the managers will post better-than-average returns and one or maybe two will post worse. Can my mother figure out ahead of time whom to bet on? Can you? Can anybody? Buffett? Munger? Soros?

So to summarize: If my mom invests on her own, my sister and I will need to have a long talk with her. A loooong talk. If she uses an index fund, she'll earn market returns. If she divides her money up equally among the three financial gurus, again, she'll earn market returns. If she tries to pick the right horse, she might outperform, she might underperform.

Some sharp-minded critics may argue that my illustration is slightly flawed because of subtle nuances like blah, blah, blah, blah, blah. Whatever. Its basic teachings hold true.

To outperform the market's return, you have to outperform the majority of others who are also trying to outperform the market's return.

I've always been surprised at how few people realize that.

When you hand over your hard-earned savings to a professional money manager you deem smarter than yourself, be careful. Because you have the option to buy an index fund and match the market's return, it's irrelevant if he or she is smarter than you. Instead, what matters is whether he or she is smarter than most of the other people who are smarter than you.

Sorry, that came out rudely.

Before you move on to the next two chapters, it is imperative that you understand this one. Reread it if you're struggling. Phone me if you have any questions. Yes, I mean it.

And the math is even more fascinating in the next chapter! How can that be? What a page turner!

When Average Isn't

THE LAST CHAPTER HAD A MAJOR weakness. Beyond the writing. The analysis left out a key component. One that affects investment returns dramatically and thus alters the math behind each of my mom's choices.

Costs.

Warren Buffett, Charlie Munger and George Soros don't work for free. Nor should they. They have to charge investors enough to cover all of their expenses and turn a tidy profit. Pro bono does not a billionaire make.

Hey, even the company offering the plain, old index fund isn't giving it away. No, it doesn't need an expensive, crack research team or to compensate a high-profile stock picker, but it's not in business out of the goodness of its heart. Its shareholders want to make some money, too.

And if my mom invests on her own (heaven forbid), though she won't have to pay a money manager, she will have to deal with commissions on her trades. Plus, think of all the time she'll have to dedicate to researching. Remember, to beat the market she has to outsmart the combined efforts of the other people trying to beat the market. That's right — Marjorie Chilton has to take on and defeat the team of Buffett, Munger and Soros. Just writing that made me chuckle.

Let's look at her four choices again but now *with* costs included:

(1)   She could buy stocks on her own — such a crazy idea that I'm not even going to bother estimating her costs.

(2)   She could buy the index fund that matches the market at a cost of 0.5% a year (a typical index-fund expense ratio*).

(3)   She could place $10,000 with each of the legendary managers at a cost of 2.3% a year (a typical non-index-fund expense ratio).

(4)   She could put the entire $30,000 with one manager at a cost of 2.3% a year.

Now, if the market returns 8% over the next year, how will my mom fare under these scenarios?

Well, if Mom opts to go it alone, we won't have a happy ending.

If she buys the index fund, she'll earn a 7.5% return. That's the market's return of 8% less the cost of 0.5% charged by the index-fund manager.

If she invests $10,000 with each of the three gurus she'll earn 5.7%. What? That can't be right. But it is. As we discovered last chapter, collectively the dynamic trio *must* match the market's performance of 8%. If Buffett and Soros both earn 12%, Munger *must* earn 0%. If Soros earns 10% and Munger earns 8%, Buffett *must* earn 6%. There are an infinite number of potential combinations, but one thing is for sure: Their aggregate performance will be 8%. Of course, my mom has to pay them the 2.3% they charge, hence the 5.7% return.

Hmm.

Finally, she could choose one manager and give him the entire $30,000. Let's assume that she miraculously pinpoints the best performer ahead of time. I don't know how she does it, but she does it. Her manager posts a 9% return. His colleagues only achieve 8% and 7% returns. Mom earns 6.7% — 9% less the fund's charges of 2.3%. Disappointing! She nailed the best performer and still lost to the index fund.

Darn costs.

That was no fun. Let's go with a more uplifting version.

Mom's manager posts a 16% return! He doubles the market's return of 8% and embarrasses the other two fellows who both achieve 4%.

Now we're talking! Mom is pumped (well, as pumped as my mom gets) and earns 13.7% after costs.

It sure is lucky that she didn't pick one of the two laggards — her return would have been only 1.7% (4% minus 2.3%). Yikes. That's frustrating in a year when the market did reasonably well.

To summarize: If my mom invests on her own, it won't be pretty. If she uses the index fund, she'll earn market returns less a *small* cost. If she divides her money up equally among the three stock wizards, she'll earn market returns less a *big* cost. If she tries to pick the right horse, she might outperform, she might under-perform. But to outperform, she has to select a manager who will not only outsmart his worthy opponents, but also outsmart them by a wide enough margin to subtract the costs of 2.3% a year and still beat the index fund.

Clearly the optimal strategy for all of us, including my mom, is to invest only with the smokin'-hot-in-the-future managers.

Logically, though, that can't happen. We can't all outperform. We need a bunch of underperformers to balance the scale. Heck, we have to take advantage of somebody! Any volunteers?

Nope, the basic fact remains: Cumulatively, all of us who try to beat the market are going to tie it before we deduct costs and lose to it by a significant amount after.

The following sentence is wordy but worth the work: It's a mathematical certainty that investors who buy market-matching index funds will outperform the majority of investors who attempt to outperform market-matching index funds.

Therefore, accepting the market averages (minus a bit for costs) automatically makes you an above-average investor.

That's right — you'll beat most investors if you stop trying to.

Average *isn't*! I can see the T-shirts now:

"Average is the new fantastic!"

"Be the most average you can be!"

"Average is its own reward."

Actually, that last one's pretty good. Trademark time.

Perhaps you're thinking, "Boy, Dave is really pushing us toward market-matching index funds or ETFs with the money we want to put into stocks."

Not true. If you look back through this chapter, you'll notice that I didn't offer any opinions at all (except a few thoughts on my mom's investing skills). I just laid out the math — it did the talking.

Anyone who disagrees with the lesson here isn't arguing with me, but with some basic number crunching. William F. Sharpe, Nobel Laureate in Economic Sciences, said it well: "The conclusions [supporting trying to beat the market] can only be justified by assuming that the laws of arithmetic have been suspended for the convenience of those who choose to pursue careers as active managers."

Warren Buffett confirms: "Most investors, both institutional and individual, will find the best way to own common stocks is through an index fund that charges minimal fees. Those following this path are sure to beat the net results (after fees and expenses) delivered by the great majority of investment professionals."

Note the word "sure."

Yet it's estimated that Canadians do, in fact, try to beat the market with well over 80 percent of their stock-market money.

Some would argue it's the ultimate triumph of hope over math.

I Wish I Could Help

WE'VE NOW SEEN THAT IT'S mathematically impossible for all of us, or even most of us, to consistently outperform the stock-market averages.

But can at least *some* among us win by spotting the future mutual-fund stars ahead of time?

Maybe. But I sure can't.

And my past fund choices prove it.

It's too bad because I love doing all the research. Really. I even read the funds' prospectuses. Who does that? By the way, why isn't it prospecti? (Can you tell I'm writing this late at night?)

Early in my career, I was actually quite confident that I could predict the winners. Not perfectly, of course, but well enough to make a positive difference.

The Wealthy Barber taught readers to look for a good long-term track record; to make sure that the team who created the success was still running the show; to emphasize consistency by looking for funds that did well in both bear and bull markets; and to stay away from "fad" funds, focusing instead on value-oriented, disciplined management teams.

That still seems like sound advice. It makes perfect sense.

Doesn't work, though.

I'm forced to admit that the funds matching those criteria over the years have collectively underperformed the market. What's worse, some of the management teams in whom I was most confident have posted the weakest returns. It's frustrating, but past long-term performance has proven to have virtually no correlation to future performance. Funds with excellent 10-year track records are no more likely to outperform over the next decade than funds with mediocre results.

Sheesh.

Thankfully, today much more advanced selection techniques have replaced my rudimentary guidelines. Mutual-fund rating agencies and major investment firms have created complex algorithms and combine them with sophisticated analyses of qualitative variables. A ton of research by really clever people and high-powered computers are both involved.

I find it all very impressive.

But it hasn't worked, either.

I have yet to come across a single entity who or that can consistently pick the future champions of the mutual-fund world. That doesn't mean they're not out there. I just haven't met them. Maybe you can do it; maybe your advisor can.

I've met a phenomenal number of people, however, who can pick the *past* outperformers with uncanny accuracy.

In fact, at any point in time, most of the hot-selling funds are those with the equally hot recent performance.

But recent performance has proven to be an even less effective predictor than long-term performance. It often has a *negative* correlation to future results! Frequently, good short-term numbers are the result of the fund being overweighted in the market's surging sector. Right place, right time. Sadly, a whole whack of money flows into the fund based on its last couple of outstanding years just in time to be introduced to the financial world's greatest humbler: regression to the mean. Remember the tech bubble?

This is where the very interesting concept of *investors'* returns versus *investment* returns comes in. Over and over again, we see funds do well when they don't have a ton of assets under management, draw in big money based on that performance and *then* stumble. The funds' overall track records appear to be OK, maybe even good, but the average invested dollar got to the party late and has done poorly.

As you can imagine, I get into a fair number of debates with industry participants about our (in)ability to pick mutual funds successfully. There's a lot of money riding on clients' beliefs that their advisors can point them in the right direction. I'm sensitive to that — a lot of my best friends are advisors.

For years, I would gently try to sway opinions by talking about the formal research on the matter, the incredible challenge of overcoming high expense ratios, the math outlined in the previous two chapters, the investors'-versus-investment-return data — whatever I could. No impact. Then last year I changed my approach dramatically, dropped all the logical and math-oriented arguments and instead went with a simple question: "Do you recommend the same funds now that you did three, five and ten years ago?"

I've been impressed with how many advisors have admitted that they don't and, more importantly, have acknowledged the significance of that response.

I have absolutely no doubt that there are outstanding mutual-fund management teams out there. Even a few who will overcome expenses and put up market-beating returns over the long term.

I also have no doubt that many advisors genuinely and passionately believe they can identify them ahead of time.

I just wish I could.

Extra Caution Advised

MY SECRETARY, MAUREEN ROSS, is one of my all-time favourite people. I know it's politically correct to call her an executive assistant, but labelling me an executive is a stretch. Plus, it seems odd to call her an assistant when she does everything and I do nothing.

When I first met Mo back in the '90s, she was managing a restaurant that I frequented. We chatted often and over time I learned that she had read *The Wealthy Barber*, liked the first half, found the insurance chapter boring, thought many of the jokes were lame (some things never change!) and was annoyed that it wasn't a true story.

I'm still not sure what made me hire her.

Anyway, during one of our conversations, Mo told me that she and her husband had recently borrowed money and invested it in stocks through mutual funds. Their advisor felt it was a prudent move.

He pointed out that they could finance on an interest-only basis at seven percent — at the time, a very competitive rate. What's more, he explained, because the loan's proceeds were being used for investment purposes, the interest would be tax deductible. The after-tax cost would be only four percent or so. He finished his rather persuasive case by noting that the equity funds he was recommending had averaged 15 percent annual returns over the prior 15 years. And because the returns were made up primarily of tax-advantaged capital gains, way more than half of the growth was staying in investors' pockets.

Holy smokes, sign me up! Borrow cheap, earn big — what a great country!

Intuitively, though, we all know that it can't be that simple. There *must* be some risks. There *must* be potential drawbacks. That doesn't mean borrowing to invest is never a good idea. But you should know the full story before jumping in.

Let me start by saying that there are no hard-and-fast rules for investing success. But if there were, this would be one of them: Don't borrow money to buy an investment that has just produced an incredible 15-year performance.

Regression to the mean lurks.

That seems obvious, yet over and over again, I find many Canadians are much more comfortable borrowing to invest *after* stock markets have enjoyed big run-ups. Excited by excellent past-performance numbers and emotionally far removed from the last painful major correction, they get caught up in the excitement and assume the good times will keep on rolling.

When I first started out, I mentioned on stage one night that over the preceding few months an unusual number of teachers had asked me about taking out loans to buy mutual funds. I kidded with the audience that maybe we should all be lightening up on our stock positions: "If the most conservative investors are not only rushing in but also doing so with borrowed money, the market must be nearing a top." Soon after, a major pullback occurred.

It's a pretty sad commentary on my career that what turned out to be my all-time most insightful advice was meant as a joke.

But the more I thought about "the teacher indicator," the more prescient it seemed. So in 2007, when I again received a disproportionate number of questions from teachers about "leverage programs" (borrowing to invest), I paid attention. Having learned my lesson, I quite seriously cautioned audiences, saying, "This is hypocritical as I don't believe in trying to time the markets, but...."

Well, we all know what 2008 brought.

In 2009, as the markets bottomed out during the credit crisis, I witnessed another fascinating example of how emotions impact investing and, in particular, investing with borrowed money. I was talking to Jonathan Chevreau, the fine personal-finance columnist at the *National Post*. Although he's normally quite guarded about borrowing to buy mutual funds, he pointed out that for those who like the idea, they may never have a better opportunity. Interest rates were at multi-generational lows and unlikely to rise quickly. What's more, stock markets had been cut in half. You could finance cheaply *and* buy low. A pretty strong argument.

The very next day, I was eating lunch at Wildcraft in Waterloo (that shout-out should score me another free meal!) and bumped into a local advisor. He had been an advocate of leverage programs over the years, but said he was now avoiding them because of the market collapse.

On the surface that made no sense, yet I completely understood his position and could sympathize with it. A number of his clients had just seen the value of their portfolios fall precipitously while their debt levels stayed constant. Not a fun mix. That would upset, scare and humble any of us. The advisor wasn't being irrational. He was being human.

When it comes to the stock market, perceived risks are inversely correlated to actual risks. It's precisely when almost everybody thinks the market is safe that it isn't. And when most think it isn't that it is.

I remind myself of that constantly.

Beyond the market-timing issues, there are other potential problems with borrowing to invest. The biggest among them is the psychological pressure borrowers feel when markets struggle. Watching your funds' values fall when you have your own money invested is stressful. Watching your funds' values fall when you have the bank's money invested is incredibly stressful.

Stressful enough that it often causes sleepless nights, panicked exits or both. This is not a theoretical argument — I've seen it many times. Maureen and her husband? They're out, and I assure you, they won't be trying that again.

Figuring out how much volatility you can stomach ahead of actually experiencing that volatility is an inexact process. But for most of us, it's less than we think. And for investments made with borrowed money, it's generally way less.

One final caution: The math behind borrowing to invest isn't quite as good as it's often advertised to be. Canadian and American markets have averaged between nine and ten percent annual returns over a very extended time frame. But remember, that's before investing costs. The mutual-funds' managements have to be paid and so does the advisor. That's only fair but it obviously leaves less for the investor. Some will argue that they can pick the future outperforming funds, leading to a better return. Hey, not impossible, but for reasons outlined earlier, I think it's unlikely.

Plus, who knows what returns will be going forward? History is just that. I'm an optimistic guy, but even I'll admit that the debt situation in the developed world could create strong economic headwinds for quite some time. And with dividend yields at close to their historic lows, logically stock-market returns may be somewhat muted for the next decade or so.

But who knows? I guess that's the point: No one does. So it's probably wise to invest as though stocks are *likely* to be reasonable-to-good long-term performers but not *sure* to be.

Despite everything you've just read, I'm not always against leverage programs. I'm really not. For the right person at the right time, they can make sense. In fact, even some of the best and most conservative advisors I know have suggested them to select clients. But the approach is frequently pushed too aggressively and is clearly not for everyone. And even in cases where it may be appropriate, the recommended amounts are sometimes nutty.

Out of fairness, I should say *were* sometimes nutty. Since the recent recession, I've found the industry is suggesting much more reasonable amounts. Also, a lot of advisors have moved away from large, interest-only loans to more modest term loans amortized over 10 to 15 years. The rates are a little higher and only the interest portion of each payment is tax deductible. But most borrowers are more comfortable with the smaller debt and, as importantly, soothed by the knowledge that it is being paid down over time. A less stressed investor is a better investor.

Again, I'm not telling you not to borrow to invest. But make sure you think it through from every angle. It's another one of those ideas from the financial world that often works better in PowerPoint presentations than it does in real life.

Up and Down and All Around

YOU'LL FREQUENTLY HEAR THIS ADVICE: "Don't try to get rich quickly in the stock market — it's a fool's errand. Instead, settle to build your wealth slowly and steadily."

The first part of that counsel is unquestionably sound. The second part might appear wise, but it is impossible to execute.

Equities don't move up slowly and steadily. They don't emulate the tortoise in Aesop's famous fable, but rather a drunken version of the hare.

Stock markets race ahead, fall back, sit still, collapse again, grow exponentially, flatten out, shoot up, crash down and generally drive investors batty.

Yes, over many years, equities as a group will probably post a solid rate of return. But "steady" is not an appropriate adjective to describe their likely journey there.

Annual returns do not congregate closely around the market's long-term average. In other words, extreme years do not occur on occasion, they occur regularly.

For example, the S&P 500, the most widely used index of U.S. stocks, has been either up more than 20 percent or down in approximately two-thirds of the years since 1926. Another way to look at that is that the S&P 500 has risen between 0 and 20 percent in only one-third of the years in that period. That's hard to believe. Even financial professionals are surprised when I share those statistics with them.

Stocks have much to offer to the true long-term investor. But you can't achieve market returns without putting up with market volatility. There's no way around that. One of the best ways to help yourself handle the ups and downs is to have realistic expectations before investing.

There's no such thing as "normal" annual returns in the stock market. Steady? Not even close.

By the way, I once asked Greta, whom you met earlier, if she knew what the S&P 500 was and she responded, "Of course I do, but I'm not into car racing." That still makes me laugh.

Oblivious

"There are certain things that cannot be adequately explained to a virgin either by words or pictures. Nor can any description that I might offer here even approximate what it feels like to lose a real chunk of money that you used to own."

Fred Schwed Jr., *Where Are the Customers' Yachts?*

I'm amazed at how hard it is for all of us, including me, to stay the course when the stock market runs into tough times.

Sure, we know we need to focus on the long term. Yes, we're fully aware that panic is our enemy. Obviously, we agree that it makes little sense to sell low.

Yet, instinctively, that's what we're tempted to do.

Anything to stop the bleeding.

Many investors, pretending to act rationally, convince themselves that they'll get out now but buy back in when the market finishes its decline.

Right. Apparently the top was completely missed but nailing the bottom shouldn't be a problem. Ah, the allure and the illusion of accurate market timing.

Others offer up this unusual strategy: "I'm going to cash out now — the markets are horrible. But *after* the rebound, I'll reinvest."

Hmm. Sell low, buy high. If trying to time the market is foolish, intentionally mistiming it is downright nutty.

But it's also strangely understandable. We all fear losing money and, ironically, it's often that very fear that causes us to do so. Like most things involving discipline, riding out the storms is much easier in theory than in reality.

So, what's the most effective approach I've seen among investors who somehow manage to do it?

Steely determination? Complex risk-management strategies? Day-to-day monitoring and tinkering?

Nope. Indifference.

I'm completely serious. Many of the most successful stock-market investors I've met are borderline clueless. Some aren't even borderline.

They're often not knowledgeable investors. They're usually not passionate investors. And they're certainly not attentive investors.

They're just successful investors.

They allocate the appropriate percentage of their money to equities, commit to rebalancing their portfolios periodically and then get out of the way.

They don't follow their stocks' fluctuating prices each hour. They don't look at the net asset values of their mutual funds every day — they probably wouldn't know where to find them. Many don't even read their monthly statements.

My father is a classic example.

When I first started out, I helped him invest $25,000 in an international mutual fund. Years later, after a rare glance at his statement, he complained, "Wow, this is unfortunate — my fund's now worth only $13,500."

Something didn't make sense. I pointed out that despite a couple of significant pullbacks, overall the markets had done well and he must be mistaken. Turns out he had 13,500 units. Units, not dollars. At seven bucks each, we calculated his holding was worth $94,500.

"My, I'm doing well with this!" he exclaimed proudly.

Yep, that's my dad — master investor.

It sounds contradictory, but you can learn a lot from this man who knew so little. Ironically, investors often chase their money away by watching it too closely.

That said, I think it is important to monitor your portfolio's holdings and returns on occasion — annually would seem about right. My dad's approach of once a lifetime is a bit extreme.

Unorthodox, But...

OVER THE YEARS, I'VE SEEN SOME rather odd "systems" developed by people trying to beat the stock-market averages.

Shake-your-head stuff.

One guy picked stocks strictly based on his horoscope. As a Scorpio, I don't believe in astrology. Another bought shares only in companies headed by someone who *hadn't* graduated from university. That strategy worked well during the tech boom but not so well during the bust.

I must admit, though, that one weird idea not only intrigued me, but also stood up quite well in the real world.

A few years back, a man called our office to crow about his investment acumen. He claimed that his portfolio had beaten the market averages over an extended time period and, to top it off, it had done so with less volatility than the general market.

I was skeptical and for good reason. I've met very few people who outperform the market after costs. I've found that most who think they have, have merely miscalculated their returns.

I explained that to the caller but he insisted that his numbers were accurate. He faxed over his transaction details and I punched them into a software program. To my astonishment, his figures were bang on — he *was* beating the market!

Frankly, I chalked it up to luck but thought it polite to at least call back and ask, "What's your secret?"

"It's simple. I follow only mature Canadian companies that have established track records of paying reasonable dividends. From that group, I buy shares in firms that I do business with but hate."

I thought he was kidding but there was no accompanying chuckle. "'Hate'? What am I missing?"

"Well, if I hate these businesses but I'm still dealing with them, they must have a heck of a good situation. Obviously, I really need whatever it is they're selling and the competition can't get at them. A captive audience gives them pricing power and staying power — tough to beat!"

I was primed and ready to offer an intelligent rebuttal but nothing jumped to mind.

There's no point in naming names here and offending anyone. But you could probably guess many of the companies in his portfolio pretty accurately. Everyone else has.

Some would argue the "hate" qualifier had nothing to do with his success. Instead, it was purely a result of focusing on mature, dividend-paying companies. That group has been a strong performer in the declining-interest-rate environment of the last two decades.

But I'm not so sure — maybe he is on to something. Warren Buffett has always believed that businesses with sustainable competitive advantages offer investors the best opportunities. Look for firms with deep and wide moats around them, he says. Well, this counterintuitive approach appears to be an excellent way to measure moats. I think it's clever.

Just the same, I've never intentionally followed this unusual stock-selection criterion. You probably shouldn't either — if it ends up not working, you'll hate the companies and your port-folio and me. That's a lot of negative emotion.

Interestingly, Peter Lynch, the famous, long-retired money manager, advocated the opposite tack and urged us to buy shares in businesses we are passionate about.

I used to love eating Krispy Kreme doughnuts on the way home from Blockbuster Video.

Whoops, better to have consulted my horoscope.

A Widely Held Misconception

MEDIA TYPES SEEM TO SAVOUR this line: "Billions of dollars have left the stock market over the last several weeks."

After these news reports, people invariably ask me, "Where do you think all the money is going? Bonds? Gold? Real estate?"

None of the above.

Let's say there are one million shares of Chilton Incorporated outstanding. They last traded yesterday at $10 a share, giving the company a market value of $10 million.

Realizing that no company named after me could truly be worth that much, you wisely decide to sell your 1,000 shares. Unfortunately, it's a rough day for equities and there are no buyers at $10 a share. You're so eager to move on that you happily accept the best offer at $9.

Chilton Inc.'s market value is suddenly only $9 million.

By selling a mere $9,000 worth of stock, you've lopped $1 million off the company's market value. You've ruined the fun for all of us.

Stock prices are set not by the entire market through careful analysis and consensus building, but by the decisions of the very small percentage of owners currently looking to sell and the very small percentage of potential investors currently looking to buy.

It takes surprisingly few people — many acting on emotions instead of rational thought — to dramatically affect prices in the short run. That helps explain why stocks are so volatile. It's also a good reason to pay little attention to day-to-day price fluctuations. They're noise. As Warren Buffett's mentor, Benjamin Graham, so cleverly put it: "In the short run, the market is a voting machine, but in the long run it is a weighing machine."

It's important to understand a million bucks didn't leave the market in this transaction; only $9,000 did. And even that's misleading because $9,000 also came in from the buyer — an obvious, yet often neglected, point.

No "net" money departed the market.

So where did the million dollars in lost market value go?

Poof.

The Silent Killer

IN THE FINANCIAL WORLD, THE difference between the highest "bid" price for an investment asset (the most anybody wanting to buy is willing to pay) and its lowest "ask" price (the least anybody wanting to sell is willing to accept) is known as "the spread."

So, if you're checking out a stock and it's a $5.00 bid and a $5.25 ask, the spread would be $0.25.

Now, if you stepped in and bid $5.20, what would the new spread be? Even my sister answered $0.05.

Technically, that's correct.

But there's a much wiser way to define "the spread." A way that will help you be a better investor.

A "spread" should be described as the difference between the price you're willing to pay for an investment asset and the price the next highest bidder under you is willing to pay.

So when you bid $5.20 on our stock, the newly defined spread will be $0.20 — your $5.20 bid price minus the next highest bid of $5.00.

Why the new definition?

Well, remember that adage that something is worth only what somebody is willing to pay for it? It's valid. And that somebody isn't the person whom you're trying to buy from — he or she is obviously the seller. And once you own the something, that somebody isn't you either.

Nope, the key person is that next bidder in line. His or her offered price represents the highest value the potential buyers, outside of you, are currently placing on the asset.

Clearly, that's an important figure to know! If it's far below the price you're trying to purchase at, you may want to rethink your bid.

The importance of all this is best illustrated by a joke I heard when I first entered the business:

> A client calls his broker and asks for the market on a certain stock.
>
> "It's $1.00 bid, $1.15 ask," he's told.
>
> "Buy all you can at $1.15," he instructs the broker.
>
> "You've got 20,000 and now it's $1.15 bid, $1.25 ask."
>
> "OK, pick up as much as possible at $1.25," the client pushes.
>
> "Done. It's now $1.25 bid, $1.75 ask. Do you want me to hit the offer again?"
>
> "Absolutely!"
>
> "You bought another 60,000 shares at $1.75. It's now trading at $1.75 bid, $1.85 ask."
>
> "Fantastic!" the aggressive buyer celebrates. "Sell it all in that range!"
>
> "To whom? You're the only guy buying!" the broker responds.

That's funny, but the message is serious. Examine the joke carefully. No one else's bid changed. The second highest price offered stayed at $1.00. Again, *that's* the key figure. It would have to rise 75 percent for our frenetic buyer to sell and break even on his last purchase.

Maybe he gets lucky eventually, but that's certainly not the way to invest.

Going back to our first example, assume the seller comes down and meets your $5.20 bid. Exciting! But do you now own shares worth $5.20 each or $5.00 each? Our adage and the real world of markets both say the latter.

The bid's going to have to rise $0.20 to bring you up to even. That may not seem like much, but it's four percent — far from insignificant. And that's before commissions.

Spreads are the silent killers of investment returns. Seldom discussed, often not even noticed, they inflict great financial pain.

You can limit their damage by investing primarily in liquid markets (markets with narrow spreads) and by trading less often. Far less often.

Day trading in penny stocks?

Stop it.

A Tough Call

IN *THE WEALTHY BARBER*, THE young characters saved 10 percent of their incomes, made maximum allowable RRSP contributions, shortened their mortgage amortizations and, in Dave's case, set aside money for his child's education.

I'm not sure what stopped me from also having them cure cancer and bring peace to the Middle East.

Clearly, financial planning in the fictional world is pretty easy stuff.

In the real world, though, most of us have limited resources. We're forced to prioritize and strike balances. Figuring out how best to do that is a constant challenge.

One of the most common quandaries many Canadian families face is: "Should we add to our retirement programs or build up our children's education plan?"

That's a tough call.

Many sharp people have analyzed this dilemma carefully and pretty much all seem to have reached the same conclusion: Go with the registered educational savings plan (RESP) first until you've taken full advantage of the Canadian Educational Savings Grant (CESG). Then, if you still have some money available, contribute to your retirement plan.

Kids first. Parents second.

That blanket advice makes things very straightforward. It really should end this chapter but there's one problem: I'm not sure it's right.

Now you have a second tough call to make: Who should you trust? The brilliant, well-trained mathematical minds who've tackled this or a former cookbook publisher working with a broken calculator?

Let's take a closer look.

RESPs aren't perfect (what is?) but they're pretty darn good vehicles. The investment earnings on contributions and on grants are sheltered from tax as long as they stay in the plan. Compounding without the government grabbing its share every year is a beautiful thing.

Then when the money is withdrawn to pay for an education, the investment gains and grants are taxable in the children's hands. Now that's income splitting at its best! A young adult is likely to be in a very low tax bracket because instead of working full time, he or she is partying. Sorry, studying.

So far, so good. And it gets better!

The Canadian Educational Savings Grant mentioned earlier provides free government funding to help out. Free is excellent! The CESG will match 20 percent of your contribution to a maximum of $500 a year and $7,200 a lifetime per beneficiary.

It's hard to argue with an RESP — it truly is a great deal. Heck, you contribute $1,000 to your daughter's plan and the federal government kicks in an extra $200! What's not to like?

But remember, the original question wasn't, "Is using an RESP a wise move?" It was, "Should we add to our retirement programs or build up our children's education plan?"

These types of comparative analyses involve subjective assumptions that can influence conclusions dramatically. For example, all of the opinions I've looked at assume contributions will earn the same rate of return regardless of whether they're in an RESP or an RRSP or a TFSA (tax-free savings account). But it's reasonable to ask if the retirement saver's longer time frame would allow him or her to invest more aggressively and, thus, potentially earn a higher return.

And then there's this biggie: What if the RESP's beneficiaries don't go on to qualified post-secondary schools? You could face a major tax bill and the CESG money may have to be repaid.

This possibility is hardly a stretch — lots of kids don't pursue a higher education. Yet few of the evaluations I've examined even considered that potential scenario. I tried to, but it really does make the calculations irritatingly complex.

I used an expected-value approach based on the probability of a child attending a qualified institution. I also attempted to account for all of the other key variables, from marginal tax rates to investment returns to available RRSP contribution room for an RESP rollover. The permutations and combinations were endless.

If you're yawning right now, I don't blame you. That was not a fun weekend. Fourteen hours and six Diet Pepsis in, there was only one definitive conclusion: "I really am a loser."

The point here is that these comparisons are *always* more complicated than they seem. There are a lot of moving parts.

That said, I'll concede that the odds favour the RESP being a better mathematical move than the RRSP or TFSA as long as its beneficiaries go on to a higher education. Of course, determining the likelihood of that when they are toddlers is a tad tricky. My parents would have bet against me for sure.

But there's a much larger issue here. This is a funky comparison to begin with — it's apples versus oranges. We're not trying to determine which of two approaches is best to help us achieve the same specific goal. Instead, we're looking at two approaches matched to two distinctly different goals.

Before we even get to the math, then, we have to decide which objective is more important.

Most parents instinctively answer, "My children's education." We love our kids and naturally want the best for them. Family values, therefore, push many to opt for the RESP with their available savings.

And that's fine. I've never once been so bold as to tell someone, "I think you're crazy to put your kids' schooling ahead of your own retirement planning." But I have on occasion more softly encouraged, "If I were you, I'd build up my RRSP or TFSA instead or at least balance some retirement saving with some education saving."

Why? Because people *must* save for retirement. Especially if they're not members of pension plans. Naturally, I don't want to see young graduates loaded down with debt. But I'd rather see that than their parents struggling mightily to get by later in life.

As I said earlier, this is a really tough call.

One final point: If at all possible, try to recruit grandparents to help out with RESP contributions. Obviously, this often isn't financially feasible, but when it is, they're usually thrilled to get involved.

Admittedly, broaching this subject can be a bit awkward. My suggestion? Get some RESP brochures and say to your parents, "Here's that material you asked for." When they look confused, follow up with, "Oh, sorry, that was the in-laws." Not only do you draw their attention to RESPs, but you also create a little motivational competition and guilt.

If you're above this Machiavellian behaviour, get your spouse to do it. It's for the kids.

A Simple Idea

"DAVE, IT'S TODD. I HAVE three grand saved up in one of my accounts. I'm going to stick it in my RRSP. What should I invest it in?"

"What's your maximum allowable contribution?"

"I have tons of room available from previous years but it's irrelevant. I only have the three Gs."

"And you're sure you don't need the three thousand, or any part of it, for upcoming expenses?"

"Definitely. Totally on top of things. Gonna put the whole shot in."

"Well, you should be contributing $5,000 then."

"What!? I told you I only have $3,000. Where did you come up with *that* figure?"

"In your marginal tax bracket of around 40 percent, a $5,000 contribution will generate a refund of $2,000. Your $3,000 will take care of the rest."

"Wow, I actually understand that. But there's still one problem: Where do I get the extra $2,000 to make that big a contribution? Sure I'll get it back, but before that can happen, I'll need to put it in."

"I don't care where you get it, just get it. Transfer it from your emergency-fund account. Borrow it from your sister. Take it from your line of credit — I can't believe I just said that. Remember, you'll get it back in May or so. At five percent, the interest over four months will be less than $35. But you'll have contributed 67 percent more to your RRSP!"

"Yeah, but now I won't be able to spend the rebate I would have received from my $3,000 contribution. What's that, $1,200? Man, that would have been fun."

"True, but you said earlier that you didn't need the $3,000 or any part of it. You know you have to build up your RRSP. Well, here's a way to really get it going. Sure, you lose out on spending the $1,200, but saving involves making some sacrifices. You've already done the hard part by setting aside the $3,000 — why not take full advantage of it?"

It's so, so important to think through this fictional conversation.

Most of us save from our after-tax income. But by contributing only those after-tax savings instead of their pre-tax equivalent, we shortchange our RRSPs. And then we often add financial insult to financial injury by spending our refunds.

Obviously, that spending is sometimes unavoidable. You need the refund to cover payments that may have been pushed off while accumulating the contribution in the first place. I understand that. Life is expensive and saving isn't easy.

But 70 percent of the time when I explain this very basic strategy to people, they're keen. Like Todd, they don't need the rebate to help pay bills. They view it as found money. Yes, some diligently invest the refund or use it to hammer away at the mortgage, but most concede it usually slips between the cracks and gets spent. The only reason they haven't been using it to help them make a bigger contribution is that no one has ever walked them through the math.

For some strange reason, many advisors don't illustrate to their clients how this works. They should.

But I haven't been much better. In fact, I'm embarrassed to admit that I haven't discussed this on stage for years. There's no excuse for that as I knew it was making a considerable impact when I did.

Talbot Stevens, a financial author and speaker, deserves credit for pushing me to include this chapter. He pointed out that it's often this kind of simple idea that can lead people to saving more. Very true.

The Canadians who really get this go one step further. They figure out how much they should be contributing annually to their retirement plans and then set up a pre-authorized chequing (PAC) plan to have one-twelfth of that amount transferred monthly to their RRSPs from their bank accounts. Once that's in place, they apply to the Canada Revenue Agency for a tax reduction at source to reflect the deductible RRSP contributions.

So, using our example, Todd would set up a PAC plan for $417 a month — $5,000 a year. He'd then apply to have his tax deduction at work reduced by $167 a month. Why? Because his $5,000 contribution will lessen his taxes by $2,000 a year and that amount divided by 12 is $167. In the end, he'll have $250 ($417-$167) a month less than last year. Sounds horrible, but guess what? Over a year, that's the $3,000 he wasn't spending anyway — it's the same amount he was already saving.

How easy is that?

A larger RRSP contribution. No budgeting necessary. No borrowing required.

Love it.

Have I mentioned before that I'm a big fan of the pay-yourself-first approach?

Battle of the Abbreviations

REMEMBER WHEN LIFE WAS SIMPLE? You needed to save and invest for retirement, so you opened an RRSP and contributed as much as you could each year.

Sure, the saving part was tough. And, of course, investing always had its challenges. But at least we all knew that an RRSP was the way to go.

Everybody said so. The woman on TV. Your advisor. *The Wealthy Barber* guy. Even your know-nothin' cousin.

Then in 2009, along came the TFSA — totally fantastic savings account (or tax-free savings account).

Hmm. Suddenly, a second option to house our retirement dollars. What to do?

Many counsel us to put the maximum allowable amount into both our RRSPs and our TFSAs. For big-income, childless people living rent-free in their parents' basements, that's unquestionably solid advice.

The rest of us are probably going to have to prioritize. We need to figure out which vehicle to focus on first.

When you make an RRSP contribution, you get to deduct that amount from your taxable income. The investments inside your RRSP grow free of tax while they stay in the plan. Down the road, however, when money is withdrawn directly from the RRSP or from the registered retirement income fund (RRIF) or annuity to which the RRSP has been converted, it will be taxable.

I'm alarmed by how many Canadians still don't fully grasp that last point. Over and over again, I see net-worth statements where the full value of an individual's RRSP is listed on the Assets side, but no corresponding eventual-tax-owing amount is recorded on the Liabilities side.

You may have a $110,000 RRSP but you also have a partner — the government — waiting patiently for its share. Annoying, but true.

In essence, a TFSA is the mirror image of an RRSP. You contribute after-tax dollars. In other words, you don't get a deduction for your contribution. But once the money is in the plan, it not only grows free of tax, but also comes out free of tax. No tax ever! Fantastico!

If you don't love TFSAs, sorry, you're nuts. But that doesn't necessarily mean you should love them more than RRSPs.

When the federal government introduced TFSAs, it created a chart similar to this one:

	TFSA	versus	RRSP
Pre-tax income	$1,000		$1,000
Tax	400		N/A
Net contribution	600		1,000
Value 20 years later @ 6% growth	1,924		3,207
Tax upon withdrawal (40%*)	N/A		1,283
Net withdrawal	$1,924		$1,924

* the marginal tax rate — the rate of tax charged on the last dollar of income

I've spent almost two full books trying to avoid number-laden charts, but this simple, little table is quite illuminating. It neatly shows how a TFSA contribution is made with after-tax dollars, while withdrawals are tax-free. And an RRSP contribution is made with pre-tax dollars, while withdrawals are taxable. Yes, I've already explained that, but I thought it best to repeat.

The chart also demonstrates that if your marginal tax rate at the time of the RRSP contribution is the same as at the time of the withdrawal, TFSAs and RRSPs work out equally well.

Even the numerically challenged can understand that if the marginal tax rate is lower at the time of withdrawal than at the time of contribution, the RRSP will win. Conversely, if the marginal tax rate is higher at the time of withdrawal than at the time of contribution, the TFSA will win.

Easy, right? You just need to guess your marginal tax rate at the time of potential withdrawal and base your decision on that.

I'm so disappointed that it's not that simple, darn it. I love simple. But sadly, the real world is more complicated than the chart world. Quite a bit more complicated.

In the last chapter, we saw that many of us, if not most of us, contribute to RRSPs with after-tax savings and then spend the refund. I hope "A Simple Idea" changes that, but for right now, that's the way it is. Heck, having some fun with our refund cheque is like playing the year's first golf game or gardening on May 24th — it's an annual Canadian tradition. A rite of spring.

Let's look at a new chart that reflects that reality:

	TFSA	versus	RRSP
Contributed after-tax savings	$1,000		$1,000
Value 20 years later @ 6% growth	3,207		3,207
Tax upon withdrawal (40%)	N/A		1,283
Net withdrawal	$3,207		$1,924

Holy smokes, the TFSA is kickin' butt!

"That's not fair," you might argue. "You forgot to include the $400 tax refund that the RRSP contribution generates!"

No, I didn't. It's a chair now. Or half an iPad. Or a flight to Vegas.

And that's fine. I'm not saying it was squandered — chairs are important, especially when you're sitting. But it does mean the $400 won't help your retirement and, therefore, in this scenario, from a financial-planning perspective, the TFSA is a clear winner.

Even when we assume you'll follow the first chart's lead and contribute to an RRSP the pre-tax equivalent of the TFSA contribution ($1,000 to $600), the comparison is still trickier than it first seemed.

Why?

When you withdraw money from your RRSP or RRIF (or receive an income from an annuity to which your RRSP was converted), not only do you have to pay taxes on it, but your increased income could also lead to higher clawbacks of your Old Age Security pension, Guaranteed Income Supplement and other means-tested government benefits.

Yikes, the math here is more complex than the RRSP versus RESP debate. Way more. I don't even drink and I want a beer.

And talk about assumptions! Oh my. Go ahead: Take your best guess at what your taxable income will be 10, 20 and 30 years down the road. What about future tax rates? Will clawback rules be altered? In retirement, will you be able to income split with your spouse or will your spouse already have split with some of your income?

Wow. Maybe I should make that beer a scotch.

I've checked out a dozen analyses on the Internet and all that did was reinforce how challenging this comparison is. For example, very few factored in the effect an RRSP contribution can make on the amount of the Canada Child Tax Benefit (CCTB) parents receive. Also, almost all of the researchers assumed every dollar withdrawn from an RRSP or RRIF will be taxed at the marginal tax rate. Think about that — it's not always the case. If I have $10,000 in government-pension income and receive a RRIF payment of $53,000, it's not *all* going to be taxed at the marginal rate. In some cases, it would be more appropriate to use the average rate of tax on the withdrawal in the calculations.

That's not nitpicky — points like the last one can't be ignored. They're vital parts of the evaluation. Unfortunately.

Wake up! I'm almost done.

Based on the various assumption sets I used, the TFSA won a surprising percentage of the time (though usually not by a wide margin). In fact, for most low-income earners, it was the victor under the majority of scenarios.

That said, I frankly have no idea which way *you* should go. At the risk of being branded The Wishy-Washy Barber, I think it would be irresponsible to give a definitive "do this." Sit down with your advisor — he or she will at least have the advantage of being able to customize the assumptions to your situation. Plus, I'm sure there will soon be software or an app developed to help you figure this out. Try to curb your enthusiasm.

My final thought here is important (no, really!). TFSAs are very flexible. You can take money out of one at any time and then put it back in future years. That's being trumpeted as a huge positive by many financial writers, but it scares the heck out of me.

I'm worried that many Canadians who are using TFSAs as retirement-savings vehicles are going to have trouble avoiding the temptation to raid their plans. Many will rationalize, "I'll just dip in now to help pay for our trip, but I'll replace it next year." Will they? It's tough enough to save the new contributions each year. Also setting aside the replacement money? Colour me skeptical. The reason I always sound so distrustful of people's fiscal discipline is that after decades of studying financial plans, I *am* always distrustful of people's fiscal discipline. And even if I'm proven wrong and the money is recontributed, what about the sacrificed growth while the money was out of the TFSA? Gone forever.

Reminders: (1) If you go the RRSP route, don't spend your refund; (2) If you go the TFSA route, don't spend your TFSA; (3) Whatever route you go, save more!

"Are You Sure?"

THIS CHAPTER ADDRESSES A MISTAKE that I've seen made many, many times yet never read a word about anywhere.

Not a word.

And this mistake isn't reserved for the financially illiterate. It's an equal-opportunity blunder — even experts can fall victim to it.

Two years ago at a conference, I dipped into a breakout session where the speaker, an accountant, was wrapping up. An audience member asked a question along the line of: "If I'm saving $400 a month for my retirement, am I better to put it into a TFSA or use it to pay down my mortgage?"

The accountant's reply was something very similar to this: "They're both excellent moves. The fact is that if your rate of return on investments inside your TFSA is the same as your mortgage rate, they'll work out equally well. But, and this is key, that's only true if you don't spend the extra cash flow that results from paying off your mortgage early. You have to be disciplined and place that freed-up money into your TFSA each month. Instead of saving only $400 a month, you need to save the entire previous-mortgage-payment amount until the day it was originally supposed to be paid off. After that, you can go back to the $400 a month."

She then surveyed the group to make sure everyone understood. They all nodded.

But was her answer correct?

Obviously not, or this chapter wouldn't be here. Let me explain how the mistake was made, using an example.

Donna and Theresa are twins and as is so often the case with twins, they're the same age. They make equivalent incomes of $60,000 a year. They just bought identical homes for $250,000 each with 20 percent down payments. They both took out mortgages at 5 percent interest rates with 25-year amortizations. Their monthly payments are about $1,150.

Donna has figured out that she'll need to save $5,000 a year to fund her far-off retirement. Theresa hates math so copies that answer. Ah, but finally a difference: Donna uses her $417 a month ($5,000 ÷ 12) as extra payments against her $200,000 mortgage. Theresa contributes her $417 a month to a TFSA and invests in bonds paying 5 percent.

Twenty-five years later, the women are still twins. Donna's extra payments of $417 a month on the mortgage led to it being paid off almost exactly 10 years early. Sweet! Once it was eliminated, she started stuffing the previous-mortgage-payment amount, more than $1,150 a month, into a TFSA. (Yes, I know that eventually she'd be blocked from doing that by the TFSA contribution limits, but don't bog me down with details here or I'll talk about clawbacks again.) Like Theresa, she invests in bonds paying 5 percent.

Donna ends up at the 25-year mark with a fully paid-for home and about $180,000 in her TFSA.

But what about Theresa? She has a fully paid-for home and just under $250,000 in her TFSA.

What gives? Why aren't they tied? How does Theresa end up with so much more? Simple.

Donna neglected to also keep saving the $417 a month once her mortgage was paid off. That's where the accountant went wrong, too. She instructed her audience to contribute the previous-mortgage-payment amount to a TFSA *instead of* just the original monthly savings. But she should have said *in addition to*.

Some people find this almost insultingly obvious, but most find it counterintuitive. They argue, "Why would Donna continue to save the original amount when she's now saving even more?"

Because the truth is, she's *not* now saving even more. In fact, she's not really saving at all. Nope, she's merely reinvesting the money that she's already saved along with its return. She's taking the fruits of her 15 years of extra mortgage payments and placing them in 5 percent bonds in her TFSA. They're yesterday's news.

Think about it this way: Every dollar invested on both sides of this example has earned a 5 percent after-tax annual return. Theresa saved her $417 a month for the entire 25 years. Of course Donna's going to have to do the same to keep up. It's pretty basic stuff but the freed-up mortgage payment somehow makes it look complicated.

How common is this mistake? Incredibly common. More than half of the people whose finances I've studied who have paid off their mortgages early have been guilty of it. And the funny thing is that they truly wanted to save the appropriate amount — they just botched the math. Once they understand it, they fix the situation right away.

Well, not right away. The first thing everybody, without exception, does when I explain this to them is ask, "Are you sure?"

I sense a lot of them want to seek a second opinion.

Why doesn't anybody trust me?

It's because of Dash Lauxmont, isn't it?

The Eternal Question

"SHOULD I PUT MY SAVINGS INTO a retirement plan or use them to pay down debt?"

I don't even want to guess how many times I've fielded that question. Media members ask. Readers ask. Friends ask. Family ask. Strangers ask.

When I close my eyes at night, I hear haunting whispers from the shadows: "Mortgage or RRSP?" "Student loan or TFSA?"

It never stops! I can't escape it. It's so bad that I've actually started answering the question even when people don't ask it.

But at least I've had a lot of opportunities to fine-tune my response. This chapter might actually make sense!

And there's more good news: Building your retirement plan or paying down debt are both great options!

That said, I want to share some thoughts that may help you make the wisest choice possible.

Let's start by assuming that in your situation, contributing to a TFSA is a better move than contributing to an RRSP. (I would tell you to review "Battle of the Abbreviations," but you may not have recovered from the first reading yet.)

Let's further assume that if you select the retirement-plan route, you're not going to break into the TFSA and subvert your golden-years' funds for nefarious purposes. Like a new deck.

And, finally, let's also assume that if you opt to pay down debt, you don't make the mistake outlined in the previous chapter or spend the freed-up cash flow.

Under those circumstances, it's a pretty simple analysis. For once.

If the rate of return on the investment(s) you make with your TFSA contribution is higher than your debt's interest rate, the TFSA wins. If lower, the debt paydown wins. If the same, it's a dead heat.

So knowing that, should you contribute to your TFSA or pay down your 18 percent credit-card debt? I really hope you answered the latter. Your paydown's rate of return is the interest rate it enables you to avoid continuing to pay on the paid-down amount. By chipping away at your credit-card balance, you're earning an 18 percent annual return. Guaranteed! If you think your TFSA's investments can consistently outperform that number, you need professional help. And I don't mean professional financial help.

What about paying down your car loan versus a TFSA contribution? It depends on the debt's interest rate. If your dealership offered cheap financing at only two percent, the TFSA contribution is probably the way to go. If a traditional lender is charging you eight percent, that's a different story. Eight percent is a tough hurdle for your investment returns to jump. It's certainly not impossible, but you're going to have to take on considerable risk in your effort to do it. Most would agree that if you can grab a guaranteed eight percent after-tax annual return, you would be foolish not to take it. I'm in with the "most."

Now, what about your five percent mortgage up against the TFSA? That's a tough one.

I'll start by saying that it's never a mistake to pay down your mortgage. The after-tax rate of return is reasonable and you can't mess it up. When it comes to investing, a disturbing percentage of us mess up whenever possible. As important, making extra payments against your mortgage's principal often reduces stress and builds pride in ownership — two fantastic bonuses.

Many in the financial business concede those points but counter that an investor should be able to post a long-term performance of greater than five percent a year. They remind us that stock markets in both Canada and the United States have averaged annual returns north of nine percent since proper records have been kept.

Fair argument. I like the idea of harnessing capitalism's tremendous power through investing in a diversified portfolio of stocks. Yes, there will be lots of ups and downs (I hate the downs!), but I'm confident the returns will be solid over an extended time frame. I'm always optimistic about the long term for a very simple reason: An incredible number of brilliant people all over the world are working every day on innovative ideas to better our lives. Sounds corny, but I strongly believe in human ingenuity and creativity, and I want to own a piece of the action!

However, equities do involve risk. (Ask the Japanese.) Sure, in most instances that risk is mitigated by time, but it's still there. And don't forget that collectively we don't earn markets' returns, we earn markets' returns less costs. Certainly for the many who have mastered jumping in and out of stocks at the wrong time, the mortgage paydown looks quite smart, indeed. The hard part is admitting *you're* one of those people.

Just a few weeks ago after a speech, I was chatting with a 20-something about the retirement-savings-versus-mortgage-paydown dilemma. She was very concerned that all the debt in the developed world is going to stifle economies and hurt stock-market returns. I responded that if that's the way she felt, perhaps the mortgage paydown made more sense.

"I don't agree," she came back. "I'm young and have decades to invest. I hope the markets *do* struggle while I first start accumulating shares. I can build my holdings at good prices and take advantage of dollar cost averaging just like *The Wealthy Barber* teaches."

The "Marginally Wiser" part of this book's subtitle has now officially been called into question.

Another alternative is to diversify by strategy. That's a fancy way of saying invest for growth inside your TFSAs with a portion of each month's savings and put the rest against your mortgage. A number of my friends do that and I'm fine with it. More than fine, actually. As I mentioned earlier, it's prudent to invest as though stocks are *likely* to be reasonable-to-good long-term performers, but not *sure* to be.

One move that usually doesn't make a whole lot of sense is to choose the TFSA contribution over the mortgage paydown but then invest the contribution in guaranteed investment certificates. Most of the time, the GIC rate will be lower than the mortgage's interest rate and therefore the paydown would have provided a better return. Still beats not saving at all, though.

If you have a variable-rate mortgage, and thus a lower rate, the paydown obviously offers a lesser return. But remember, that return will float with the debt's interest rate. It's strange how few people think about that. If, over time, your variable rate moves from three percent to seven percent, your paydown's return on investment goes along for the ride. In other words, paying off even a low-interest-rate mortgage may end up being a clever move if rates rise significantly.

Lately, I've run into a number of people who have stretched their finances to the max to take on the biggest mortgages they qualified for. In most of those cases, I would aggressively push them to prioritize paying down the debt, at least in the mortgage's early years. I'm extremely worried that higher interest rates are going to dangerously pinch this group. If rates climb too much, forget not being able to save, these people may struggle to pay their bills. Even many who have locked in their rates for several years could be in trouble. With 30- and 35-year amortizations, very little principal is paid off in the first few years. At renewal, the new, higher rate could be a huge problem. Some say, "Not to worry — just tap into the TFSA." But what if the investments inside the plan happen to be down in value when they're needed? Sadly, forced sales and Murphy's Law always seem to walk hand in hand.

OK, we need to look at one more important angle. We assumed that in your situation contributing to a TFSA is a better move than contributing to an RRSP. But what if that's not the case? What if the RRSP is the more sensible path?

I hate to do this to you, but we have to take a quick second look at a chart from "Battle of the Abbreviations."

	TFSA versus RRSP	
Pre-tax income	$1,000	$1,000
Tax	400	N/A
Net contribution	600	1,000
Value 20 years later @ 6% growth	1,924	3,207
Tax upon withdrawal (40%*)	N/A	1,283
Net withdrawal	$1,924	$1,924

* the marginal tax rate — the rate of tax charged on the last dollar of income

It's kind of neat what's really happening here. In essence, with the RRSP you get to invest your $600 *and* the government's $400, for a $1,000 total. Years later, on withdrawal, you keep your part (tax-free like the TFSA) but you have to give the government back its share, 40 percent. It makes sense that the RRSP and TFSA approaches end up tied.

But if you pay a higher tax rate on the RRSP withdrawal (including clawbacks) than the tax rate at which you took your original deduction, you have to give the government not only its share, but also some of yours. Drag. That's why, when that happens, the TFSA wins — with it, you get to keep all of your share.

If, though, you pay a lower tax rate on the RRSP withdrawal (including clawbacks) than the tax rate at which you took the original deduction, you get to keep not only all of your share, but also some of the government's part! Nice. The TFSA can't compete with that. And a mortgage paydown may have trouble competing, too.

The bottom line is that when you can withdraw from an RRSP at a lower tax rate (including clawbacks) than you took the original deduction at, RRSPs are awesome. Don't let anyone tell you differently. Unfortunately, as we've discovered, divining your tax rate at withdrawal ahead of time is tricky business.

Financial expert Malcolm Hamilton is an actuary and partner with Mercer in Toronto. He is one sharp guy. He was the Gold Medallist in Mathematics in university (I wasn't). Yet when he is asked about mortgage paydowns versus RRSP and TFSA contributions, he pushes people away from the comparative numbers and advises that either move is excellent and to get at it. Procrastination is the enemy!

"Should I pay down my mortgage or fund my retirement plan?"

Yes. Immediately.

Unbowed

MORE THAN TWO DECADES LATER, I still can't believe how annoyed a number of insurance agents were when *The Wealthy Barber* hit the shelves. Roy Miller recommended term policies to the characters in the book and, wow, was that poorly received by some in the industry.

In fact, that's a major understatement. A few agents were so enraged, they spread a rumour that I had gone bankrupt following my own advice. A couple of others claimed that I was in a U.S. prison, guilty of fraud.

A lot of agents agreed with my perspective and most of those who didn't were very professional about it. However, the bad apples caused me *much* stress. I laugh about it now, but at the time I wasn't too happy with people being told I was behind bars. It got so bad, I had to threaten to sue if the nonsense didn't stop.

The culprits responded by moving away from false stories and instead told any clients who quoted the book that I was an idiot. Knowing several friends would be more than happy to provide my accusers with supporting evidence, I dropped the idea of going to court.

Well, many years have passed and I remain unbowed. I'd *still* advocate term insurance for the three characters in *The Wealthy*

Barber and, more importantly, for the vast majority of Canadians who need life insurance.

The crazy number of product names aside, life insurance really comes in just two basic flavours: term and cash value.

With a term policy, you're buying coverage for a stipulated time frame. If the insured dies during that "term," the beneficiaries collect the policy's face value. If not, they don't.

Doesn't get much more straightforward than that.

A small percentage of insurance agents think this type of policy is a horrible idea. I actually got heckled by one of them while delivering a speech years ago. "Term insurance is a rip-off!" he yelled. "If you don't die, your premiums are gone and you have nothing to show for them. Why would you suggest something so stupid?"

Man, this guy didn't know who he was messing with. Had he not heard about my prison background?

Anyway, I politely asked if he had fire insurance on his home. When he confirmed he did, I posed the obvious next question: "By your logic, isn't that 'stupid'? If your house doesn't burn down, your premiums will be gone and you'll have nothing to show for them."

He sat back down and grumbled something about me being an idiot. Why is that always the fallback position?

Cash-value policies (including whole life, universal and variable) are a combination of life insurance and a savings component. No problem there. A lot of us need life insurance and almost all of us need to save. A cash-value policy helps us achieve both objectives.

But is it the most efficient way to do so?

All insurance is really term insurance when you think about it (and for your sake, I hope that's not often). The odds of you dying at any point, obviously, aren't affected by the type of policy you own. Therefore, when you purchase a cash-value policy, each year the issuing company must extract a mortality charge — a de facto term-insurance cost — from your cash value. The rest of the money in your accumulation account can be invested in a variety of ways depending on the type of policy.

But there are several reasons why bundling term insurance with your savings and investments might not be your most prudent course, including: (1) The mortality charges (i.e., the term-insurance premiums) levied inside cash-value policies are almost always more expensive than pure term-insurance premiums quoted in the marketplace; (2) The available investments also usually involve higher fees than most equivalent ones available outside of cash-value plans; (3) Although cash-value policies do offer a tax-deferral opportunity, TFSAs and RRSPs are even more tax-efficient homes for your investments.

What does it all add up to?

If you need life insurance, I still think your best move is to buy a term policy until you've taken full advantage of TFSAs and RRSPs and until you've paid off your consumer debts and mortgage.

If you find yourself in the enviable position of having accomplished all of that, some cash-value policies may be worth exploring. Even then, though, make sure you watch your costs — they can turn a theoretically good idea into a bad one in practice.

By the way, I've read this chapter to some of the smartest actuaries I know, Malcolm Hamilton included. All of them, even those who work for major insurance companies, agree with it.

And, no, none of them are in jail.

A Big Step

HOW IS YOUR ADVISOR COMPENSATED? How much did you pay last year for the advice you were given? How has your portfolio performed over the years?

Blank stare.

That's the response I get from more than 80 percent of the people to whom I pose those questions.

The financial-advice business must be the only business in the world where most customers aren't told what they've received or how much they've paid for it.

Perhaps they have been getting excellent counsel for a good price, but how would they know?

It's nothing short of bizarre. Consider this scenario:

NHL Franchise Owner: "How much are we paying our coach?"

Team General Manager: "I have no clue."

NHL Franchise Owner: "Well, is he at least doing a good job? What's our record like relative to expectations? To objectives? To other teams'? To our last coach's?"

Team General Manager: "Those are great questions. I haven't really looked at our win-loss situation,

> though. I don't want to get caught up in all of that — I'm sure everything is fine. And he's a heckuva nice guy."

Silly, obviously. Performance and costs matter.

But to evaluate them, you need to know them.

Currently, our government and the financial industry are working together to raise Canadians' financial-literacy levels. I'm all for that. So, let's take a big step forward by providing *all* clients with clearly stated, detailed performance figures and cost breakdowns for their investment accounts on an annual basis.

Clients deserve it.

Good advisors want it.

Common sense dictates it.

Potpourri

1. Watch *Inside Job*, the Oscar-winning documentary on the credit crisis. It may sound boring, but even my kids enjoyed it. That's saying something.

2. Ellen Roseman of the *Toronto Star* and Moneyville.ca is one of my favourite financial journalists. She can write intelligently about any money matter, but I particularly like her consumer-advocate pieces. Her columns are entertaining and full of practical advice. Another person I really enjoy and who is a great teacher of "live within your means" is Gail Vaz-Oxlade, author and TV host of *Til Debt Do Us Part*. Her aggressive, in-your-face approach is precisely the wake-up call that many need. She intimidates me.

3. If you're buying stocks directly in individual companies as opposed to through a fund or ETF, be careful. Very careful. The speed and ferocity of competition nowadays is nothing short of scary. A company that looks solid and promising one day can be rocked the next by a new technology or an innovative idea from a formerly unheard-of firm located in some far-flung region. Remember, when you invest in a company, you're really buying your share of the discounted value of the firm's future profits. I would argue that it's getting harder and harder to make a reasonable estimate of what those future profits will be.

4. If that's not bad enough, it's become nearly impossible to decipher the financial statements of many public companies. Modern firms are incredibly complex entities, often with operations all over the world. Their *auditors* get fooled regularly, for crying out loud — what chance do most of us have?

5. If you insist on building your own equity portfolio instead of using a mutual fund or ETF, it's probably wise to emphasize companies that consistently pay a healthy dividend. Cumulatively, that group has tended to outperform non-dividend-paying stocks and be less volatile. Nice combination. Will that outperformance continue? I wish I knew for sure, but I think the odds favour it. Dividends have been a key and underrated part of North American markets' total returns over the decades. As the British used to say: "Milk from the cows, eggs from the hens. A stock, by God, for its dividends."

6. I've also found that investors with diversified portfolios of dividend-paying stocks are generally less likely to panic during market pullbacks. Soothed by the lower volatility and the ongoing dividend stream, they often stay the course when tough times hit.

7. I love the concept of DRIPs — dividend reinvestment plans. Many companies throughout the world, including here in Canada, offer investors the option to reinvest their dividends into more shares. More often than not, there are no commissions involved and sometimes the shares are purchased at a discount to prevailing market prices. Also, several discount brokerages are now joining in and helping clients establish DRIPs in a consolidated account. Forced saving, compounding, zero to low costs, convenience — gotta love it!

8. *The Little Book of Big Dividends* by Charles B. Carlson is a worthwhile read. Loads of common sense and some well-explained dos and don'ts of investing in dividend-paying stocks.

9. Rob Carrick of *The Globe and Mail* and Jonathan Chevreau of the *National Post* should be on your must-read list. They're experienced columnists who are very passionate about helping Canadians with their personal finances. They don't pull any punches! I think both of our national newspapers have outstanding teams of money-management columnists. Am I just saying that in a desperate effort to garner rave reviews for this book? Well, I'm not above that behaviour but, no, I really mean it.

10. If you have a group RRSP at work and your employer matches all or part of your contribution, take advantage of it! I spoke for a firm several years ago that matched dollar for dollar the employees' contributions, and 25 percent of its workers still weren't signed up. They were turning down an instantaneous 100 percent return! I'm not even sure what to say about that.

11. In the mutual-fund world, you'll often hear the term MER. It stands for management expense ratio and represents the annualized percentage of a fund's assets that unitholders pay to cover management charges, administrative expenses, distribution fees and operating costs.

12. The distribution-fee portion of the MER is, in essence, the ongoing commission paid to your advisor. In other words, his or her compensation is embedded in the MER rather than billed directly to you. So, if an equity fund's MER is 2.3 percent and the distribution fee is 1.0 percent, you're really paying 1.3 percent to the fund's management company for its services and 1.0 percent to your advisor for his or her financial-planning advice and mutual-fund recommendations.

13. Is your advisor worth one percent? I have no idea. Many are. Many aren't. You already know that I don't believe advisors are any better than the rest of us at picking future outperformers among the mutual funds. So I think it comes down

to their financial-planning guidance. Has your advisor helped you develop a plan? That's obviously key! Does he or she offer tax advice? Assess your insurance needs? Work with you to build a portfolio of investments consistent with your goals and risk-tolerance level?

14. The financial media often point out that commission-based compensation systems can colour advisors' judgments. That's unquestionably true and, unfortunately, I see examples of it frequently. However, it's only fair to also note that many commissioned advisors do an excellent job. In fact, lately I've read several plans produced by this group that have been very impressive. Certainly some advisors let selfish concerns influence their recommendations, but we shouldn't paint everyone with the same brush.

15. There's another problem I see almost as much as bad advice — no advice. I'm very frustrated by the number of people I meet who are paying advisors handsomely through their mutual-funds' MERs, yet almost never hear from them. And when they do, it's only to arrange to obtain a cheque for that year's retirement-plan contribution. Not good.

16. I have no issue with our financial institutions and advisors making money. Even good money. As I've mentioned, a lot of my closest friends work in the industry. But we have a wacky number of financial products in Canada that are too expensive by any common-sense measure. For example, I see some mutual funds with MERs in the area of three percent. Anybody who thinks that's a fair deal for clients has a fundamental misunderstanding of arithmetic, markets' returns or both. Yes, that was uncharacteristically blunt.

17. Many advisors are moving to a fee-based model. Some charge a flat or hourly fee but most charge a percentage of assets. This model takes away the potential conflict of interest of the commission-based model and its costs are more transparent. I think we'll see a lot more of it going forward.

However, for clients with low-turnover portfolios, the old-fashioned, commission-based model may be a better deal. No one approach is best for everybody.

18. I'm not good at making predictions. Well, actually I am — I'm just not good at making accurate predictions. Here's one I'm very confident in, though: Over the next few years, the costs of financial products and financial advice are going to go down significantly. Competition is heating up and consumers are becoming better educated — a powerful combination.

19. I had always struggled for a response when people asked me how to find a good advisor. Then, about a year ago, a woman posed the question in a slightly different manner: "What are the common denominators among the better advisors you've crossed paths with?" Hmm, that got me thinking and I was surprised that three things really jumped out at me: (i) The best advisors are excellent communicators. They know how to listen, how to teach and how to coach; (ii) They love to read about all things money. That's probably a big part of how they developed their strong communication skills; (iii) They spend their time developing and implementing sound financial plans, not trying to outsmart the stock market. Tough to overstate the importance of this last observation.

20. Both Dianne Maley of *The Globe and Mail* and Andrew Allentuck of the *National Post* examine a specific family's finances each Saturday. Lots of good information packed into short reads. I love the way the two writers, and the advisors they consult, aren't afraid to tell it like it is.

21. It's surprising how many financial plans I see where a family's entire RESP is sitting in cash, earning almost nothing. Hey, being conservative is one thing, but all cash? That's crazy. They should at least buy some GICs to bump up their rate of return.

22. Please keep your will updated. It's ridiculous how many otherwise-responsible people don't. It doesn't take a lot of time or money, but it can make a *huge* difference for your loved ones.

23. Do not draft your own will! An experienced lawyer will not only help you avoid mistakes, but will also raise issues you probably wouldn't consider on your own. While I normally push you to watch your costs, in this case, don't be "penny-wise, pound-foolish."

24. Think *very* carefully when selecting your executor. It's a seriously difficult job — one that requires a unique combination of smarts, strong attention to detail and good people skills. (Rules out my editors — let's see if that makes it to print.) Don't just default to your best friend or adult-aged children.

25. For heaven's sake, make sure your family and executor know where to find your will. It's incredible how often wills go missing. Also, always keep a copy at your lawyer's office.

26. A will is revoked by marriage unless it states that it's being signed in contemplation of that marriage. Yikes, can you imagine how much trouble this little-known fact can cause when people with children get remarried?

27. Read *The 50 Biggest Estate Planning Mistakes...and How to Avoid Them* by Jean Blacklock and Sarah Kruger. It's exceptionally well done.

28. When you're analyzing your life-insurance needs, keep in mind that we're in a low-interest-rate environment. Too many Canadians are assuming that they'll be able to earn eight percent on the insurance proceeds that result from a family member's death. Unlikely. This mistake is leading a lot of families to buy less coverage than they should.

29. There are some truly great financial blogs aimed at Canadians — too many to cover here. But I do want to mention four that I think you'll benefit from visiting regularly. Squawkfox.com is a wonderful site. Its lone blogger is Kerry Taylor. She's a woman after my heart, combining insightful savings tips and a nice sense of humour. Canadian Capitalist.com is run by Ram Balakrishnan and is nothing short of outstanding. He's an excellent writer and covers off a bunch of interesting and relevant topics. WhereDoesAllMy MoneyGo.com, written by Preet Banerjee, is another very worthwhile stop. He looks at a wide variety of subjects, often from unique angles. Preet is much smarter than I am and a better dresser. I don't like him. Finally, Canadian Business.com/author/larrymacdonald is extremely well done. Larry is a former economist, but don't hold that against him. I like his writing style and read his pieces often. The comment sections on these blogs are fantastic. Most of the readers posting opinions are really knowledgeable and represent very practical perspectives. I've learned a lot from reading them.

30. My favourite tax-planning book is *101 Tax Secrets for Canadians* by Tim Cestnick. Updates are released every two years and Tim is somehow able to make the read enjoyable. OK, tolerable. Fine, not miserable. I mean, it is tax planning we're talking about here. Excellent stuff.

31. The older I get, the more I push people to diversify *very* broadly when investing. No one can consistently be at the right spot at the right time. And even if someone could, he or she would be smart enough not to share the information with the rest of us.

32. I'm always cautioning audiences not to pay attention to economic forecasts, so I'll admit it's hypocritical of me to offer this one up: The developed world's debt levels are going to subdue its GDP growth for a considerable time.

This means we should diversify not only among individual securities and asset classes, but also by investing in various geographic regions. It also may be wise to lower your projected portfolio returns. (Let's hope I'm wrong...again.)

33. I have no idea what to tell the young people currently looking to buy houses in Toronto or Vancouver. I don't envy them. Yes, low interest rates are helping to keep debt-servicing costs down. But those same low rates have played a major role in pushing home prices to crazy levels relative to incomes. The high cost of living in those cities is making proper financial planning difficult, even for the disciplined. New buyers are being *forced* to stretch and then trying to survive until their rising incomes give them a fighting chance to save. Not ideal.

34. I've always been surprised (very surprised) at how few seniors are purchasing annuities. Many retirees don't have work-related pensions and it makes sense that they should "pensionize" some of their savings by creating a guaranteed monthly income. Having that income not only takes away the risk of outliving their money, but it's also psychologically comforting. Why don't more older Canadians look at this product? Well, some are waiting for higher interest rates. Most, though, are fearful that they will "get hit by a bus" right after the purchase and forfeit their monies to the insurance company. However, there are lots of ways to build guarantees into the product to protect against that (the immediate forfeit, not the bus). By the way, deal only with the top-rated companies — annuities are no good if the insurance company dies before you do! Also, even though I think annuities are underutilized, don't go overboard here. Annuities are appropriate for a percentage, not all, of retirement portfolios.

35. I'm frequently asked how often I push "pay yourself first" to my own kids. People question, "Have they tuned you out

yet?" Yes, but not for that reason. I honestly don't preach that to them much. Thankfully, I don't need to — neither one is much of a spender. They're not stuff-oriented at all. I'll admit, though, I do constantly remind them to always live in homes that are modest relative to their incomes. Scott has proven he's a good listener by taking up residence in my basement.

A Man With a Plan

WHEN I FIRST ENTERED THE financial business (no, it wasn't in the 1940s), I had an encounter that has influenced my thinking tremendously. In fact, it's had more impact on me than any of the books I've read or seminars I've attended.

At the time, I was a stockbroker and wrote monthly articles for a local business publication, *Exchange Magazine*. An area farmer in his early 50s, I'm guessing, dropped by my office. He said that he enjoyed my "unusual writing style" (I'm not sure what he meant by that) and wanted to see what I thought of his financial plan and investing approach.

"I don't have it written down so I'll just tell it to you," he began.

Uh-oh. I'm always genuinely happy to help, but I had visions of being trapped for hours listening to an itemized summary of his portfolio and the reasoning behind each position.

"My wife and I use pre-authorized chequing to put as much as we're allowed to into RRSPs every year. I use a spousal plan for some of my contribution dollars so that we'll end up with about the same amount of money under each of our names. We want equal incomes in retirement for tax reasons."

I was going to break in to confirm all that made sense, but wasn't given the opportunity.

"I put half our **RRSP** monies into GICs. Lately, I've been going longer term because rates are high, but I usually spread it out so that I have money coming due every year. The other half I put into stocks of big Canadian companies and we're into dividend reinvestment plans where possible.

"Outside the **RRSP**, any extra money we've had we've put down on our debts. Two years ago, we finished paying off our mortgage.

"Since then, I've used the extra cash to help out our son at university and to start picking up some shares in stable companies like the banks and utilities.

"We have our will updated and a term-to-100 insurance policy to cover off the taxes our estate will owe on the farm when we die.

"That's it. Nothin' fancy."

I've seen thousands of financial plans over the years. Some have upward of 50 pages. Spreadsheets, pie charts, complex forecasts and detailed recommendations have been woven together and spiral bound with a fancy cover.

Few, though, have been better than the farmer's.

I'll admit that I'm biased by my affection for simplicity. However, over the years, I've relayed this plan to many of the sharper financial minds I know and they *all* agree it was excellent.

Now, obviously, no single plan is well suited to everyone, so don't run right out and emulate this one. But there's a lot more to learn from this chapter than first meets the eye.

The farmer and his wife lived within their means. They used forced saving. They took advantage of RRSPs and compounding. They kept costs down. They took the long-term view.

"Nothin' fancy," indeed. Roy Miller, the wealthy barber, would approve.